ADVANCE PRAISE FOR

Looking Backward and Forward: Policy Issues in the Twenty-first Century

"[In]. . . this collection . . . lie many solid insights and thoughtful gems. Though written over a number of years, unlike other commentators Wolf has no subsequent need to make major adjustments in his views or eliminate internal conflicts, for these papers demonstrate a very high degree of consistency. Some, like his very useful analysis of the probabilistic nature of intelligence, need to be taken to heart by passing critics. The special value of his observations is that he is never caught up in the prevailing fashions of the day. When a forecast fails to materialize, he is the first to recognize it. Would that other commentators followed this practice."

James Schlesinger, *former secretary of defense, and former director of Central Intelligence*

"In a world of conventional wisdom, Charles Wolf is a rare original thinker whose essays are replete with lucid analysis that yields gems of wisdom mined from across our political, economic, and foreign policy landscape. The essays are also wonderfully readable."

Karen Elliott House, *former publisher of the* Wall Street Journal *and a RAND trustee*

"Charlie Wolf's wisdom, experience, and prescience distinguish him as a rare talent. In his latest collection of essays, *Looking Backward and Forward*, he offers valuable insights into today's global challenges."

Donald Rumsfeld, *former secretary of defense*

"Charlie Wolf's collection of essays is readable, educational, and provocative. With careful analysis and logic, he explodes myth after myth. He grades himself and fully deserves the high marks most of his op-eds receive."

Frank C. Carlucci, *former secretary of defense*

"It is a rare pleasure to peruse a collection of essays which are easy to read yet highly instructive. Every one of Charles Wolf's essays deals with recent events, yet his explanations are helpfully anchored in history. It is as if we are being offered rich tutorials on important public policy issues. We are being taught how to take a balanced view of the political aspects of each issue, so as to rise above the inevitably quarrelsome nature of politics. And we are also being taught how to benefit from the best advice that an economist can offer, because Charles Wolf knows how to weave his knowledge of economics into the cultural and social context."

> **Fred C. Iklé**, *a distinguished scholar at the Center for Strategic and International Studies and former undersecretary of defense for policy*

"Charles Wolf's *Looking Backward and Forward* is a joy to read. In this collection of brief essays, Wolf applies the rigorous logic, relentless empiricism, and contrarian outlook of a skilled economist to challenge conventional wisdom on a host of contemporary foreign policy issues."

> **Michael H. Armacost**, *the Shorenstein Distinguished Fellow at the Asia/Pacific Research Center, Stanford University*

"If you want reasoned, informed and often contrarian essays on some of the most important topics of our time, this is the book for you. China is vulnerable on many fronts but is resilient; comfortable but slow-growth Japan might experience a wake-up shock from China; here are Russia's economic pluses and minuses and much more. Nuggets of value abound."

> **Henry S. Rowen**, *senior fellow, Hoover Institution; professor emeritus, Graduate School of Business, Stanford University*

"Harry Truman longed to meet a one-handed economist and Charlie Wolf is his man! These delightful essays are wonderfully direct, and Wolf's astute prescriptions stand the test of time."

> **Gary Hufbauer**, *the Reginald Jones Senior Fellow, Peterson Institute for International Economics*

"Charlie Wolf has a special talent for combining rigorous logic with hard data and fresh insight, spanning the fields of security, development, and the international economy."

> **Bruce Berkowitz**, *research fellow at the Hoover Institution and author of* The New Face of War

LOOKING
BACKWARD
and FORWARD

LOOKING BACKWARD *and* FORWARD

POLICY ISSUES IN THE TWENTY-FIRST CENTURY

Charles Wolf Jr.

HOOVER INSTITUTION PRESS
Stanford University Stanford, California

www.hoover.org

Hoover Institution Press Publication No. 560

Hoover Institution at Leland Stanford Junior University, Stanford, California, 94305-6010

First printing 2008
15 14 13 12 11 10 09 08   9 8 7 6 5 4 3 2 1

Manufactured in the United States of America

The paper used in this publication meets the minimum requirements of the American National Standard for Information Sciences—Permanence of Paper for Printed Library Materials, ANSI/NISO Z39.48-1992.♾

Library of Congress Cataloging-in-Publication Data
Wolf, Charles, 1924–
Looking backward and forward : policy issues in the twenty-first century / by Charles Wolf Jr.
     p.   cm. — (Hoover Institution Press publication ; no. 560)
  Includes bibliographical references and index.
  ISBN-13: 978-0-8179-4871-9 (cloth: alk. paper)
  ISBN-13: 978-0-8179-4872-6 (pbk: alk. paper)
  1. Economic policy. 2. Foreign economic relations.
3. Foreign relations. I. Title.
HD87.W65 2008
330.9—dc22   2007030582

Contents

Foreword

How many times have you read an op-ed in the newspaper that changed the way you think? Most of us would answer, not very often. But if you were lucky enough to read an essay by Charlie Wolf in the *Wall Street Journal*, the *Los Angeles Times*, or the *International Herald Tribune* (or other major publications) in the last few years, your perspective was enlarged and your thinking was enriched.

This is the third collection of Charlie's essays, following two successful publications in 1991 (*Linking Economic and Foreign Policy*) and 1997 (*The Economic Pivot in a Political Context*), published by Transaction Publishers. It has been my privilege to contribute the Foreword to all three, probably because it was at my urging years ago that Charlie publish his work outside RAND, where I first met him. These twenty-five essays were written between 2002 and 2007 and, like good wine, are getting better as he ages.

With his global perspective, Charlie explains such mysteries as Chinese-style capitalism, Japan's relationship with North Korea, what if Iraq had not been invaded, and how to improve public diplomacy. My own favorite is the last essay in this book, "Liberals and Conservatives: Who's What and Where?" in which

Charlie observes that "the policy orientations associated with liberals and conservatives in American politics are the precise opposites of what the labels stand for in the rest of the world." Think that one over.

A fine mind coupled with clear writing skills is a treasure. Readers of Charlie Wolf's latest work will find rich rewards indeed.

Newton N. Minow

Preface

The twenty-five essays in this book were written between 2002 and early 2007. With a few exceptions, they were published in the *Wall Street Journal*, the *Wall Street Journal Asia*, the *Wall Street Journal Europe*, the *Los Angeles Times*, the *International Herald Tribune*, the *South China Morning Post*, the *Japan Times*, the *International Economy*, *Policy Review*, and the *Milken Institute Review*. The unpublished essays were presented as dinner talks or were circulated privately. One of the essays, "Public Diplomacy" (chapter 24, pages 121–148), was coauthored with Brian Rosen. All of the essays are collected in this book in the hope that the whole may exceed the value of the scattered individual chapters. All of the essays are printed as originally written with only light editing by the Hoover Press.

Toward this end and to make their disparate content cohere somewhat more closely, I've divided the chapters into five sections dealing, respectively, with *China* (chapters 1–7), *Other Asia* (chapters 8–10), *Other Regions* (chapters (11–16), *The Global View* (chapters 17–20), and *The United States* (chapters 21–25).

The subjects dealt with in these geographic areas span or at least touch on a wide range of economic, political, security, and diplomatic issues. The stance generally adopted in each essay is to consider a then-current issue—whether in China or Japan or Iraq or Russia—from the standpoint of its precursor context and its prospective consequences, hence, the *Looking Backward* and *Forward* of the book's title.

A few themes, often contrary to conventional wisdom, emerge for the reader's consideration and perhaps disputation. For example, I suggest that, under not implausible circumstances, rapid and full convertibility of China's currency might lead to its depreciation rather than appreciation; that China's remarkable economic performance is both likely to be sustained and to confront enormous and possibly disruptive impediments in its efforts to do so; that "unilateralism" in U.S. national security policy may sometimes be preferable to multilateralism; that, despite presumptions to the contrary, the United States is as or more disposed to favor multilateralism than are many other countries; that the erroneous expectation that Iraq possessed nuclear weapons does not imply that the prior intelligence leading to this expectation was flawed; that U.S. coalition "partners" may have interests and behaviors more congruent with those of the United States than do putative U.S. "allies"; and that the ability of the U.S. economy to adjust to a reduction of its chronic current account deficits may exceed the ability of countries such as China and Japan to adjust to reductions in their chronic current account surpluses.

The variety and complexity of these themes, as well as their common characteristic of spilling over the standard boundaries of political, economic, and military affairs, will be the typical pattern associated with policy issues in the twenty-first century—hence, the book's subtitle.

I have always felt that commentators—whether they be the regular hired columnists of the major news media or the occasional, often more academically credentialed volunteers—should be held to account for the accuracy of their pronouncements. Without jeopardy to First Amendment sensibilities, such accountability might be provided by some type of scoring system devised by outsiders or even by the authors themselves. Although, in the latter case of author judgment, the possibility of a culprit serving as his own juror might lead readers to doubt the objectivity of the results, even the subjective ex post assessment would discourage hyperbole before the fact and encourage responsibility afterward.

With this aim in mind, I have added a brief "Postaudit" at the end of each essay indicating whether, in my judgment, the argument set forth is currently valid and relevant, compared with when it was written. In my perhaps biased assessment, nineteen of the essays stand up to this test quite well (each receiving an A or A−), four do passably well (receiving Bs), and one doesn't make the cut (receiving a C). Of course, the reader is welcome to make her own independent assessment, as well!

Charles Wolf Jr.
Santa Monica, California
July 2007

PART ONE
China

1. Capitalism, Chinese Style

ALTHOUGH THE PARTY FAITHFUL still refer to China's economic system as a "social market economy with Chinese characteristics," a more apt description is a "mixed state and private economy with *European* characteristics." These characteristics include a pervasive, interventionist government role as producer, regulator, and corporate owner; a growing and innovative private business sector (currently producing more than one-third of China's non-agricultural output); and a variety of joint ventures between government, domestic, and foreign business. (Two of these characteristics also bring to mind the formerly stagnating economy of Japan.)

What Britain's prime minister, Tony Blair, has referred to as the "Third Way"—supposedly something between central planning and American-style capitalism—and Germany's chancellor, Gerhard Schroeder, described no less elliptically as the *Neue Mitte* ("New Middle"), both embody those mixed attributes that increasingly apply to the Chinese economy.

A slightly edited version was published in *The International Economy* in winter 2002 under the title "Capitalism, Chinese Style."

Two recent developments, in addition to China's admission to the World Trade Organization, indicate the direction in which China's economy is evolving: first, efforts by the China Securities Regulatory Commission (CSRC) to reform China's dysfunctional stock markets; second, the recent welcome extended to private businesspeople to become members of China's ruling Communist Party.

Bringing the Shanghai and Shenzhen stock markets up to speed is a requisite for sustaining, in the future, China's past high economic growth rate. China has the world's highest savings rate—more than 35 percent of annual GDP, compared to less than half that rate in most major economies. Effective securities markets help guide savings into efficient and profitable investments, but this vital function has not been performed effectively in China. Instead, so-called policy loans to state-owned enterprises (SOEs) have been provided by the state-owned banks, in the process siphoning capital that could otherwise be available to non-state enterprises were securities markets more ample and more effective. In fact, China's securities markets have been thin and their trading volume low. One indicator is the small proportion of GDP represented by the market capitalization of stocks listed on China's markets (by comparison, in the United States the market capitalization of listed stocks is more than twice U.S. GDP).

To expand and improve the operation of securities markets, the CSRC (China's counterpart of the Securities and Exchange Commission in the United States) confronts two major problems: (1) continued government holdings of two-thirds of the voting shares of the "privatized" former SOEs among the 1,100 companies listed on China's exchanges and (2) the failure of corporate governance of the listed companies to contribute to improving the functioning of equity markets.

To remedy these deficiencies, the CSRC has made several important market-oriented reforms. First, government holdings are being gradually reduced, although the pace has been constrained by a fear that the markets would be destabilized if the pace were accelerated. This dilemma—rapidly reducing government holdings, without unduly destabilizing the markets—is perhaps more tractable than has been assumed. For example, a portion of the government shares might be converted to nonvoting preferred stock and transferred to the state banks, thereby offsetting some of the nonperforming loans on their fragile balance sheets, while extruding the government from intervention in corporate management.

Second, the CSRC has encouraged the listing of new nonstate companies, adding about a hundred new listings annually—a rate that should accelerate if and as new companies meet the financial and other standards set by CSRC for initial public offerings (IPOs).

Third, the CSRC has been making serious efforts to educate corporate management, as well as both government and retail shareholders, about the importance of improving corporate governance to enable securities markets to function more effectively.

Improved corporate governance is essential to make management accountable to prospective shareholders and thereby motivate savers and investors to acquire securities, thus widening and deepening the markets. This requires increased transparency in corporate management, frequent and regular financial reporting in accord with rigorous accounting standards, and the appointment of independent (nonaffiliated) members to corporate boards, audit committees, nominating committees, and compensation committees, practices far removed from the familiar practices of business management in China. Where ownership remains predominantly in the hands of the Ministry of Finance and other government ministries that hold majority shares in listed companies, management remains beholden to those entities and the interests of *retail* shareholders are largely ignored. Maximizing shareholder value is typically not high among the objectives of government owners.

Another indicator of China's circuitous path toward a more market-oriented system is Jiang Zemin's decision on July 1, 2001, to open the way for new entrepreneurs to become party members. (Before that, several thousand businesspeople were already among the party's 65 million members, but most of them became members when they were employed by the state—for example, by SOEs, by state ministries, or by the military.) The July 1 decision anoints "new" capitalists as potentially acceptable party members, thereby overriding the deeply ingrained ideological stance against the profit-oriented business class, which was previously viewed as something to be resisted rather than embraced.

In the short run, Jiang's decision is no less significant as a symbol than as a significant reflection of accelerated market-oriented reform. Probably the number of capitalists admitted to party membership in the next year or two will be relatively limited to forestall opposition by leftists in the party to this "anointment" of capitalists. In the middle to longer run, however, the pace will quicken, and capitalist membership in the party will swell along with the burgeoning of private business in the Chinese economy. Hence, the policy influence of the business sector is likely to increase significantly in the future. One consequence will be greater pressure to strengthen the rule of law as a precondition for economic performance and for the growth of the business sector. Another consequence is likely to be enhanced pluralism within party councils, reflecting the diversity of business interests across a wide range of economic and regulatory policies and practices.

The vector of near-term and longer-term changes under way in China's economy suggests something more like the mixed system of Europe's "New Middle" economies, rather than a prototypical American system. To be sure, the economic performance of the European economies has been something less than lustrous, and it is at least debatable as to whether the expanding reach of the European Union's bureaucracy is more likely to improve than to impair it. But in China the prospect that a mixed system involving both government intervention and private capitalism will enhance economic performance may be brighter. Unlike Europe, China's economic system is moving away from the heavy hand of centralized state planning toward a system marked by greater openness, competitiveness, and flexibility.

POSTAUDIT

With few exceptions, the main points are as valid now as when the article was published in 2002. Some exceptions are that the growth of the market-oriented private sector has been even more rapid than the essay anticipated (the private sector accounted for 60 percent of China's GDP in 2006) and that improvement in corporate governance has probably been somewhat less than envisaged.

---

2. Foreign Investment Leverages China's Growth

AMONG THE FEW PROPOSITIONS on which all China experts—those in China as well as outside—agree is that foreign direct investment (FDI) has been one of the two or three most important contributors to China's rapid economic growth during the past fifteen years. Initial calculations suggest that each $10 billion of FDI is associated with between 0.9 percent and 1.6 percent of annual economic growth in China. If annual FDI fell by $30 billion, China's annual growth might decline by nearly half its current rate.

FDI is defined as the creation and/or acquisition, by foreign capital owners, of tangible assets situated in the recipient country.

There is less agreement concerning the explanation for FDI's impact. According to one view, the effect of FDI lies in its packaging of technology, management, and marketing (especially export marketing), together with capital, with each component enhancing the effectiveness of the others.

A second explanation contends that FDI's effectiveness results

Published in the *Asian Wall Street Journal* on June 24, 2004, under the title "Uncertain Times for Foreign Investment in China."

from the preferential treatment it is accorded, enabling FDI to take advantage of opportunities within China inaccessible to domestic capital due to barriers to capital mobility that exist among China's thirty-one provinces.

In any event, China is the second-largest recipient of FDI in the world economy (the largest is the United States). The $43 billion of FDI in China in 2001 is larger than the corresponding amounts received by all other Asian economies, excluding Hong Kong, which functions as an entrepôt for FDI in China as well as other Asian countries. FDI in China has risen to this level from a figure of $2 billion in 1986, increasing at a compound annual rate of more than 18 percent, and steadily rising from 1986 through 1997, with a slight decline since 1997 in constant 1995 US dollars.

The consensus among China experts is that FDI will continue to rise in the coming decade. According to a survey I conducted a few months ago, 88 percent of the respondents expressed this view. But experts are typically more reliable in interpreting and explaining the past—for example, in their consensus that FDI has been crucial in contributing to China's economic growth during the past fifteen years—than in forecasting the future. In forecasting what *will* happen, rather than explaining what *has* happened, their testimony has frequently been wrong. Consider, for example, the failure to forecast Japan's stagnation in the 1990s against its background of remarkable growth in the 1970s and 1980s; the failure to predict the plunge in the economies of Korea, Indonesia, and Thailand in 1997–1998; or the protracted slow growth of Germany in the 1990s.

So, although FDI may remain at high levels or increase in the coming decade, it may also fall substantially, with serious consequences for China's economic growth. This uncertainty is due to the many factors—both within China and outside—that can affect FDI in an upward or downward direction.

Internal factors prominently include such political developments as the harmony or friction that accompanies the impending transition from China's third-generation to its fourth-generation leadership and the prevalence of political and social stability in China or, conversely, the spread of civil unrest from rural areas to urban areas.

Numerous other factors will make China's economic environment either congenial or adverse for FDI in the coming decade. These include, for example, whether China moves toward or away from a rule of law in which property rights are respected and predictable, equities markets are expanded, corporate governance becomes more responsive and transparent, and corruption recedes rather than advances. The outlook for FDI in China will also be materially affected by the pace and fidelity with which China complies with its WTO commitments, whether the Chinese yuan remains stable while moving toward full convertibility, and whether and how the huge volume of nonperforming loans on the balance sheets of China's four state banks continues to grow without triggering a financial crisis.

With increasing integration and competitiveness in global capital markets, FDI in China will depend not only on these internal factors but on how the environment for FDI evolves in other parts of the world in both capital-exporting countries (such as the United States and the European Union), as well as capital-importing emerging markets including Korea, Russia, Eastern Europe, Southeast Asia, Taiwan, South Asia, and Latin America. Hence, China's ability to attract FDI will depend on other countries' political stability; their development and protection of property rights, corporate governance, the rule of law; and their possible resource discoveries, in particular. It will also depend on China's ability to maintain reasonably harmonious relations with its neighbors, including the United States, Japan, the European Union, Taiwan, and Southeast Asia.

In the past, FDI in China has been sparked by the lure of its potentially huge market. In most instances, promise has exceeded performance. Thus far, few FDI undertakings have resulted in significant profits for foreign investors. As a consequence, some of the previous optimism has been replaced by increasingly hard-headed calculations of costs and prospective returns.

In sum, future FDI in China will depend to a much greater extent than in the past on China's risk-adjusted, after-tax return on investment, relative to opportunities elsewhere in a world of globally integrated capital markets.

The ensuing stakes for China are immense. If the combination of internal and external factors influencing FDI in China moves in an unfavorable direction, China's forgone economic growth would be seriously eroded. This prospect will and should, as Samuel Johnson observed, "concentrate the minds" of China's policymakers.

POSTAUDIT

The importance ascribed to FDI was right on; the prognosis was way off! FDI in China has continued to grow but at a decreasing rate.

---

3. Fault Lines in China's Economic Terrain

BETWEEN 1980 AND 2002 China's annual economic growth was 8.6 percent. Despite some fuzzy statistics, as well as ups and downs along the way, this remarkable record overshadows Japan's economic "miracle" of the 1970s and 1980s by nearly 75 percent: Japan's average annual growth in the 1970s and 1980s was 5 percent.

If China is able to sustain its growth at a rate similar to this recent history (its current rate is reported as 8.1 percent), its gross domestic product by 2025 would be only modestly below that of the United States, although its *per capita product* would still be less than 15 percent of that of the United States.

This rosy scenario confronts an array of potential "fault lines"—obstacles that could seriously hinder or even reverse this trajectory. Eight potential fault lines are especially serious. They impend in a wide range of differing sectoral and institutional areas, constituting serious obstacles to China's future growth. These

A slightly edited version was published in the *Los Angeles Times* on June 1, 2003, under the title "Pitfalls on Path of Continued Growth," and in the *South China Morning Post* on August 7, 2003, entitled "Eight Threats to China's Economic Miracle."

fault lines, together with rough estimates of how much they would reduce China's annual economic growth, can be briefly described as follows:

- *Unemployment, poverty, and social unrest* Open and disguised unemployment in China amounts to more than 20 percent of the total labor force, or approximately 170 million people. Recent and prospective increases in unemployment are due to population increases in the 1980s, privatization and downsizing of inefficient state-owned enterprises, and the employment effects of China's efforts to comply with its WTO commitments. Rural poverty is accompanied by increased income inequality between rural and urban areas, by rural-to-urban migration, by rising urban unemployment, and social unrest. A possible worsening of these adversities could cause a reduction of between 0.3 and 0.8 percent in China's annual growth during the coming decade.

- *Corruption* Pervasive and perhaps increased corruption in China could adversely affect China's economic growth by distorting resource allocations, though how large these distortions would be is difficult to estimate. In cross-country comparisons, increases in corruption are associated with lower rates of economic growth. Were corrupt practices in China to worsen, China's position would decline in the country indexes that link economic growth with a prevalence of corruption. Such an adverse shift could reduce China's expected annual growth rate by perhaps 0.5 percent.

- *HIV/AIDS* Various estimates place the prevalence of HIV/ AIDS at between 600,000 and 1.3 million, with an annual rate of increase between 20 and 30 percent! Plausible projections of these trends would seriously affect China's economic growth through the costs of treatment and through reductions in factor productivity and per capita output. In "intermediate" rather than "pessimistic" scenarios, annual deaths from HIV/AIDS would be between 1.7 and 2.7 million in the second decade of the twenty-first century, cumulating by 2020 to more than 20 million and associated with annual reductions in China's GDP growth of between 1.8 and 2.2 percent in the period from 2003 to 2015.

- *Water resources and pollution* China is beset by a maldistribution of natural water supplies. North China, with more than 33 percent of China's population, and at least an equivalent share of its GDP, has only 7.5 percent of naturally available water. South China typically has an abundance of water, sometimes accompanied by serious floods. Pollution discharges from industrial and other sources aggravate the water shortage for consumers and industry in the North. Whether China's policymakers push for less efficient, capital-intensive water transfer projects from South to North or opt for more efficient recycling as well as conservation of water supplies in the North, will significantly affect future growth. Resolving this allocation issue is complicated by political considerations involving the relative influence of provinces in the North and the South. If economically inefficient policy decisions are made, China's expected GDP growth would be reduced by 1.5 to 1.9 percent in the coming decade.

- *Energy consumption and prices* China has shifted from being a net exporter of oil in the early 1990s to importing nearly half its oil and nearly a fifth of its natural gas. The major risk posed for China's sustained growth in the energy sector, however, does not depend on its increased oil imports but on the prices at which oil and natural gas are available. If there were a major and sustained contraction in global oil supplies and a sharp increase in oil and gas prices lasting for a decade, the bottom-line effect on China's annual growth would be a reduction of between 1.2 and 1.4 percent.

- *Fragility of the financial system and state-owned enterprises* The fragility of China's state-dominated financial institutions is suggested by the high volume of nonperforming loans (NPLs) on the balance sheets of China's four major state banks that are a result of "policy lending" by the state banks to loss-incurring state-owned enterprises. Estimates of total NPLs vary enormously, but they may amount to more than 60 percent of China's GDP. Under not implausible circumstances, China could experience a panic run on the banks, large-scale capital flight, a significant reduction in savings, and a sharp decline in capital formation. The ensuing financial crisis and credit squeeze could lower annual GDP growth by at least 0.5 to 1.0 percent.

- *Possible shrinkage of foreign direct investment* In the past fifteen years China has experienced a steadily rising volume of annual direct foreign investment (FDI), reaching $50 billion in 2002, significantly boosting China's economic growth. Although a high volume of FDI may continue in the future, there are plausible internal as well as external circumstances under which it might contract. Adverse *internal* developments include possible future tensions following the so-far smooth leadership succession, the possibility of internal financial crisis, and the inconvertibility of the renminbi (RMB); *external* impedance might result from improvements in the investment climate in Eastern Europe, Russia, Indonesia, India, and other countries that compete with China for foreign capital. A recent RAND study estimated that a reduction of $10 billion a year in FDI may be associated with an expected reduction of China's annual GDP growth of between 0.6 percent and 1.6 percent.

- *Conflictual adversities: Taiwan and other potential conflicts* Although the status quo in cross-strait relations between

China and Taiwan is broadly beneficial to the People's Republic of China, Taiwan, and the United States, tensions could escalate into possible conflict in the future, with growth-inhibiting consequences for China's resource allocations, exchange rates, and equity markets. The bottom line of these adverse developments could be a decline in China's annual growth of between 1.0 and 1.3 percent.

Were all of these adversities to occur, China's annual growth would be reduced between 7.4 percent and 10.7 percent, resulting in negative numbers for China's economic performance as a whole. Although the probability that all of these would occur is extremely low, the probability that none will ensue is also low. Moreover, the probability that several of them might cluster is higher than their joint probabilities would suggest because of interdependencies among them. For example, an internal financial crisis would likely have negative impacts on foreign direct investment, on unemployment, and on corruption.

The ramifications of these eight fault lines are likely to extend into all levels of China's society, government, and party structure. To mitigate the ensuing stresses will demand an enormous and continuing set of consultations, negotiations, and transactions among China's central and provincial governments and its party apparatus. This demanding process will probably preoccupy China's new collective leadership during the next decade, predisposing it to avoid external distractions and perhaps especially to maintain equable relations with the United States.

POSTAUDIT

The eight fault lines remain but, like those in California's tectonic plates, have not shown signs of near-term eruption.

4. China's Currency Dilemma and How to Resolve It

CHINA'S CURRENCY VALUATION elicits growing criticism and resentment among some policymakers in the United States and also generates controversy and confusion among policymakers in China. But there is a way of resolving the dilemma—standing pat versus revaluing—that would be sensible and beneficial all around.

That the partly convertible Chinese yuan (equivalently know as the renminbi—literally "people's currency") is now and has been tightly pegged to a fully convertible U.S. dollar is itself an anomalous situation. "Partial convertibility" means that, whereas holders of liquid yuan assets can use them to purchase current imports of goods and services from abroad, they cannot normally use yuan to purchase foreign stocks, bonds or for direct investment abroad.

From the point of view of American critics of China's currency peg, the fact that the U.S. bilateral trade deficit with China in 2004 was $160 billion, whereas two-way trade between China and the United States was nearly $220 billion (China's imports

A slightly edited version was published in the *Asian Wall Street Journal* on May 20, 2005, under the title "A Sensible Solution to Beijing's Yuan Dilemma."

from the United States were less than $30 billion) suggests that the yuan is *under*valued, that the tight peg of 8.28 per yuan per U.S. dollar indicates that Chinese policymakers are manipulating the yuan's value to the detriment of U.S. exports, and that the yuan should be revalued or the dollar peg removed.

China's trading partners in Asia and Europe are no less critical of the yuan's dollar peg, although they are less vociferous than the U.S. critics, preferring to let the United States do the heavy lifting on this matter. Because the dollar's value has declined relative to the euro and the yen in global exchange markets, other countries whose currencies' values float criticize China's dollar peg because it effectively *depreciates* the yuan relative to nondollar currencies. As a consequence, the exports of those countries are less competitive with China's exports than they otherwise would be, whereas China's exports to those countries are boosted.

On the other hand, from China's point of view, criticism by other countries of the yuan's dollar peg doesn't allay worries among Chinese policymakers about altering the yuan's value. Their fear is that any appreciable change in the dollar peg might lead to still greater difficulties and more heated criticism than does the present policy. For example, if the peg were lowered by, say, 15 percent, to 7 yuan per dollar, China's bilateral trade surpluses with the United States would probably not change much nor would its global trade surpluses be much affected. Underutilized production capacity in China's booming export sector is so large that production would continue even if profit margins were narrowed. Moreover, a lowered peg would likely increase China's imports of oil and metal ores, adding further demand pressures to those already-inflated markets and generating additional criticism of China by other consumers. Chinese policymakers also fear that, were the peg to be changed, the effect would be to attract "hot" money into China in anticipation of further adjustments in the future, thereby contributing to inflation and overheating of the Chinese economy.

Finally, and probably most significant, if China were to allow the yuan's exchange value to float while maintaining its blocked capital account, pressure to make the yuan fully convertible could grow. In each of the past two years China has allowed about $4–5 billion of capital export transactions, for the purpose of acquiring particular foreign assets favored by China's policymakers—such as oil refineries and high-tech industry (for example, the Lenovo acquisition of IBM's PC business). These transactions, however, are only a drop in the bucket. Behind them loom liquid deposits in the major Chinese banks of more than 21 trillion yuan, or more than 180 percent of China's GDP. The holders of these huge yuan assets include business enterprises, urban and rural households, agricultural deposit holders, and other entities. If as much as 10 percent of these holders of yuan assets were to seek to diversify their portfolios by acquiring foreign assets, the yuan might as likely depreciate as appreciate relative to the U.S. dollar!

Resolution of China's currency dilemma lies in synchronizing two policy changes: (1) a further unblocking of China's capital account and (2) a broader float of the yuan on foreign exchange markets. China's current account surpluses would continue to generate a large supply of foreign currencies; substantially unblocking the capital account and allowing convertibility of between 5 and 10 percent of liquid bank deposits would generate additional demand for them. China's huge foreign exchange reserves ($660 billion) would provide an adequate cushion for any short-term volatility that might ensue.

By allowing a partial and gradually rising proportion of liquid yuan assets to be freely convertible into dollar, euro, and yen assets, China's policymakers would contribute measurably to improved efficiency in the allocation of the Chinese economy's large capital resources and at the same time contributing to more effective functioning of the global economy and neutralizing the foreign critics of China's currency policies.

POSTAUDIT

The analysis and policy perspective remain valid, notwithstanding that China has devalued the yuan by a cumulative 5 percent, with its peg to the dollar allowed to fluctuate around a narrow 1–2 percent band.

---

5. More about the Chinese Currency

IN THE DEBATE OVER China's exchange rate policy, overwhelming if not exclusive attention has been devoted to one argument that is erroneous, whereas a second argument that is valid has been virtually neglected.

The erroneous argument is that China's failure to revalue its undervalued currency, the yuan—also known as the renminbi (RMB), literally "the people's currency"—is responsible for substantial loss of U.S. jobs, especially in manufacturing.

The error of this argument lies in the fact that the loss of American jobs over the past few years—about 700,000 through the first three quarters of 2003—is directly attributable to something that is paradoxically part of the innovative character of the American economy and has hardly anything to do with China or any other of America's major trading partners. This "something" is the growth of U.S. labor productivity at an annual rate of about 4 percent. Productivity growth at this high rate means that, as a result of better equipment, training, and management, the level

A slightly edited version was published in the *South China Morning Post* on September 26, 2003, under the title "Behind the Rhetoric."

of employed labor that produced last year's gross domestic product could produce 4 percent more this year. In fact, the rate of growth of the U.S. economy in the past year has been about 3 to 3.5 percent, which means that employment has decreased by about 0.5 percent—namely, the 700,000 jobs referred to above.

So China's currency value really has nothing to do with the explanation of the so-called job-loss recovery of the U.S. economy.

The valid, but neglected, argument about China's currency is that China's failure to move from partial convertibility of the yuan (confined to conversion for current trade in goods and services) to full convertibility (including international capital transactions) is responsible for misallocation of China's own capital resources as well as the inability of China's policymakers, no less than of their critics, to estimate the yuan's "true" exchange value.

The yuan's "worth" in terms of the market basket of goods and services it can buy—what economists refer to as its "purchasing power parity"—is at least 40 percent greater than the 12 U.S. cents that is the nominal exchange value of one Chinese yuan (i.e., 8.3 yuan per U.S. dollar). Of course, the relevant market basket referred to here includes many categories of goods and services that are not internationally tradable—such as domestic personal services, real property, construction, and so on—and hence do not affect international transactions and payments or the nominal exchange value of the yuan.

However, capital transactions definitely do affect, often decisively, nominal exchange rates. For example, if holders of dollar or yen assets wish to invest in China, they can use those assets to buy yuan, thereby tending to prop up the exchange value of the yuan. On the other hand, if holders of yuan assets wish to acquire dollar or yen assets—for example, equities, bonds, property—they are unable to do so because the yuan is not convertible for such capital transactions. China allows, indeed encourages, foreign capital to flow in but prevents ordinary domestic Chinese capital from flowing out.

The principal exception to this impedance has been the use by China's Central Bank of the economy's surpluses on its current account transactions to purchase U.S. treasury bonds, thereby adding to China's official foreign exchange reserves. In the past four years China's reserves have grown from $168 billion in 2000 to $357 billion in 2003.

Thus if the individuals, households, and companies in China that hold trillions of yuan in bank deposits or other repositories wanted to diversify their holdings, hedge their risks of yuan holdings, or simply seek higher returns by acquiring dollars, euros, or yen assets, they are blocked from doing so because of the yuan's inconvertibility for normal capital transactions.

It is impossible to determine the extent to which holders of yuan would want to buy foreign assets that they are precluded from doing now. Some rough guesses, however, can be made. For example, China's aggregate savings rate of 30–35 percent annually—the highest of any of the major national economies in the world—means that its annual savings amount to about 3.5 trillion yuan, about $420 billion, an accumulation over the past four years of about 1.6 trillion yuan in bank deposits in China since 2000. If as little as, say, 2 percent of these holdings—a figure approximately equal to the percent of annual savings in Japan that is devoted to acquiring foreign equities, bonds, and other foreign assets—it would not be implausible to expect that purchases of foreign assets by Chinese holders of yuan deposits could be in the neighborhood of $32 billion, were the yuan to become convertible on capital account.

The outflow of capital from China that would be triggered by full convertibility of the yuan could thus exceed China's diminished current account surplus with the rest of the world. As a result, the yuan might not implausibly *depreciate*—that is, become less expensive relative to the dollar or euro—as it would be to appreciate. In any event, the real foreign exchange value of the yuan can only be determined *after* it becomes fully convertible, not just partially so as it is at the present time.

POSTAUDIT

With the passage of time, the numbers have changed (e.g., China's foreign exchange reserves and current account surpluses have grown enormously), but the core analysis and policy prescription remain essentially valid.

6. Two Major Problems Confronting China: One Hard, the Other Harder

AMONG THE MAJOR ECONOMIC PROBLEMS confronting China, two are particularly difficult. The problem that has lately received the most attention and concern is actually the less difficult of the two. The second not only is more difficult but also has been largely ignored in public discussion.

The easier problem is the so-called overheated Chinese economy and the worry that the "bubble" may burst, with serious consequences for Asia and the world economy.

China has achieved and sustained a remarkably rapid rate of economic growth—9.2 percent in 2003 and an annual rate of 9.7 percent in the first quarter of 2004. Along with rapid GDP growth have come various indicators of overheating, including a 3.5 percent increase in the consumer price index in the first quarter of 2004 on a year-over-year basis, a 20 percent rise in the money supply in 2003 partly due to foreign capital inflow, and a $30 billion jump in China's foreign exchange reserves.

At China's Boao economic forum in April, President Hu Jin-

A slightly edited version was published in the *Asian Wall Street Journal* on July 7, 2004, under the title "China's Rising Unemployment Challenge."

tao explicitly acknowledged the overheating problem but expressed confidence that it can be controlled and a "hard landing" avoided. There are reasonably strong grounds for his confidence. Awareness of the problem by China's top policymakers is an encouraging sign, as is their recognition of the various policy instruments they can employ in a timely manner to forestall and mitigate the problem. These instruments include raising interest rates, boosting capital and reserve requirements in the four main state banks, and installing and enforcing more-rigorous standards of risk assessment for bank lending under the guidance of China's Banking Regulatory Commission.

China's monetary policymakers are reluctant to push these instruments too hard lest they overshoot and, in the process, precipitate a sharp fall in the economy's performance. Instead, curbs have been imposed on bank lending in certain overheated sectors, including steel and automobile production. These modest, piecemeal efforts seem to be having a cooling effect: growth both in the money supply and in bank lending has been lowered by 2 or 3 percent in the past few months, although consumer prices continue to rise. In any event, if the limited measures invoked thus far turn out to be insufficient, prudent use of the other policy instruments should enable the brakes to be applied without producing a hard landing. Although China isn't out of the woods yet with its overheated economy, the problem appears manageable.

The problem that is more difficult to resolve springs from a dilemma presented by two economic objectives, both of which are of crucial importance for China's future: (1) sustaining a high rate of economic growth and (2) generating ample job opportunities for large numbers of unemployed and underemployed workers. For political and social as well as economic reasons, achieving a high rate of job creation is no less important than is sustaining a high rate of GDP growth.

Although the two objectives are usually viewed as compatible and even mutually reinforcing, there is a fundamental tension arising between them because of the two-sided effects of rising labor productivity.

GDP growth is enhanced by boosting labor productivity, but the employment-generating effects of GDP growth, per unit of growth, are *lowered* as labor productivity rises. Stated another way, increased labor productivity—defined as output per worker or per hour of labor—is of central importance in propelling economic growth, but, the more rapidly labor productivity increases, the less new employment is created by economic growth.

According to conventional wisdom, China's huge (1.3 billion) population provides a virtually inexhaustible supply of low-cost labor that, along with more-globalized markets, presents strong competitive challenges to industries and firms in other countries. What is less well recognized is that globalization also creates a serious challenge for China and its policymakers. For China to sustain a high rate of economic growth, it must combine labor with technology, management, design, and marketing, as well as capital. The effect of this combination will be to raise the productivity of labor substantially and continually, thus reducing significantly the added employment generated by economic growth.

The rate of increase in employment is precisely equal to the difference between the rate of GDP growth and the rate of growth in labor productivity. If and as labor productivity rises, generating a specified number of additional jobs requires a still higher rate of GDP growth.

During the four-year interval between the end of 1998 and the end of 2002, China's GDP rose from 7.8 trillion yuan ($946 billion) to 10.6 trillion yuan ($1.28 trillion), in constant prices, an annual increase of 7.8 percent. During the same interval, labor productivity rose from 11,100 yuan to 14,380 yuan per worker, an annual rate of increase of more than 6.7 percent. According to China's official statistics, employment during the four-year period rose to 737 million from 706 million, an annual increase of 1 percent.

Thus, whereas China's economy was growing at the highest annual growth rate (7.8 percent) of any of the world's principal economies, its increase in employment was only 1 percent annually.

China's employment problem is even more serious than these numbers suggest. Notwithstanding the reported increase in total employment of 31 million between 1998 and 2002, registered urban unemployment increased to 4 percent from 3 percent—to 10 million from 6.7 million—whereas urban employment was growing to 248 million from 224 million. Thus, the number of new urban jobs was 10 million less than the number of workers seeking them.

These numbers are only the tip of the unemployment iceberg. Research by RAND indicates that, when proper allowance is made for "disguised" rural unemployment as well as "unregistered" urban unemployment, China's actual unemployment rate soars to an estimated 23 percent of the total labor force. (The term *disguised* unemployment refers to labor that is reported as nominally employed but in fact does not add to output—in the U.S. labor market, *featherbedding* is the nearly equivalent term.)

The strains and stresses that will result from the persistent masses of China's unemployed and underemployed labor are difficult to assess but hard to overestimate. China's employment problems are a deeper, more long term, and potentially more serious challenge to economic and social stability than is the temporarily high temperature of its economy.

POSTAUDIT

China's overheated economy has cooled a bit, consumer prices have been rising, and its unemployment problems remain acute, as argued in the essay.

7. U.S.-China Relations: Mostly Partners, Sometimes Rivals

U.S.-CHINA RELATIONS, and the respective national interests that underlie them, are generally harmonious. The usual harmony, however, is occasionally jarred by sharp dissonance. Currently, the dissonance arises from legislation pending in the U.S. Congress to pressure China to raise substantially the value of its putatively "misaligned" yuan relative to the U.S. dollar. The United States' aim is to reduce China's large current account surplus with the United States (nearly $200 billion in 2006), which, it is contended, is appreciably affected by China's deliberate policy of undervaluing the yuan.

The internal American politics behind this measure are complex if not obscure—for example, the legislation is sponsored by both the Democratic chairman and the ranking Republican member of the Senate's Finance Committee but is opposed by other members of both parties. In any event, its economic logic is basically flawed.

The source of China's global surplus and its smaller but still

A slightly edited version was published in the *South China Morning Post* on August 2, 2007, under the title "A Few Low Notes Won't Spoil US-China Harmony."

relatively large surplus with the United States lies in the excess of China's huge domestic savings rate (more than 35–40 percent of its approximately $5 trillion GDP) above its high but lower domestic investment rate (about 35 percent of GDP). The American economy is characterized by a precisely opposite imbalance: an excess of gross domestic investment (about 14–16 percent of its approximately $12 trillion GDP) over domestic savings (about 10–12 percent of GDP, entirely due to retained corporate earnings and depreciation allowances because household savings are close to zero and government dissaving is about 2–3 percent of GDP).

If and when these basically symbiotic imbalances become unsustainable, tinkering with the yuan/dollar exchange rate will have little relevance or influence. Quite different policy changes will be required if, for example, the U.S. savings rate is to be boosted by two or three points and China's savings rate is to be lowered by several points. Moreover, if these changes are to be accomplished without in the process triggering recession in the United States and inflation in China, the exchange rate will be the result, not the cause, of the necessary changes.

Beyond the symbiotic relationships between the two economies, the national interests of both countries are in close harmony. Both China and the United States have major interests in maintaining and enlarging a global trading system that is free and open and encouraging global markets that allow free capital flows in both directions, facilitating American investment in China and Chinese investment in the United States.

As the world's first- and second-largest importers of oil—U.S. daily imports are 10 million barrels; China's are half as large—the United States and China have convergent interests in increased and diversified sources of oil supply as well as moderate and relatively stable oil prices. Both countries also share a strong interest in developing efficient alternatives to fossil fuels through expanded production of nuclear, solar, and biomass energy.

Energy represents a divergent as well as a convergent interest between China and the United States. The more hydrocarbon fuels each of them consumes, the more global oil prices will tend to rise to the detriment of other consumers. China's subsidies to household and state enterprise consumers of energy thus harm energy consumers in the United States. As major consumers in the same market, China and the United States are rivals as well as partners.

Convergence between Chinese and American national interests extends to major issues of international security as well. Both countries have vital interests in nonproliferation of nuclear and other weapons of mass destruction. North Korea's nuclear test in October 2006 concerned China no less than it concerned the United States. Moreover, China's influence has been crucial in inducing the DPRK to resume the Six-Party Talks and in forging a promising if slippery agreement for halting and then dismantling North Korea's nuclear programs.

Confronting nonproliferation in Iran, China's interests are less congruent with those of the United States. Iran is a major source of China's oil imports, as well as a growing market for China's exports. Those commercial interests, in combination with its perhaps not unrelated disposition to believe that Iran's progress toward weaponizing nuclear technology is far behind that of North Korea, incline China to be less cooperative with the United States in pressuring Iran to reverse its nuclear programs than in the case of North Korea.

The threat of Islamic terrorism and the compelling importance of combating it are of deep concern to China as they are to the United States. China's concern is heightened by the jihadist threat posed by the separatist Moslem Uigur minority in Xinjiang province—a concern closely aligned with that of the United States.

Convergent interests in counterterrorism impel both the United States and China to share intelligence, to track and interdict financial transactions that may support terrorism, and to cooperate in other ways, including China's informal assistance in the Proliferation Security Initiative launched by the United States in 2003.

To be sure, China and the United States see other security issues in a different light. They include China's military spending (increased by 18 percent in 2007) and its investment in advanced military technology, as evidenced by China's effective antisatellite missile test in 2006. These divergences also include China's dissatisfaction with U.S. preferential treatment of India's nuclear development and U.S. concern over China's harsh human rights policies within China, as well as China's declaratory policy of using military force against Taiwan if the "renegade province" were to declare its independence.

In the broad score of major international concerns of the United States and China, harmony predominates over dissonance. That there are, nevertheless, important entries on both sides of the score recalls an observation by F. Scott Fitzgerald about the criterion for a first-rate mind: "the ability to hold two opposed ideas in the mind at the same time, and still retain the ability to function." Whether the minds behind the respective policies of the United States and China will measure up to this exacting test is an open question.

POSTAUDIT

Written in mid 2007, the ensuing interval is too short for the piece to claim much prescience. Nevertheless, I would expect that the ledger described here will have considerable validity in the longer term, subject, of course, to the caveat expressed in the concluding sentence.

PART TWO

Other Asia

8. Japan's Comfortable Stagnation

ECONOMIC STAGNATION IN JAPAN is uniquely compatible with generally prevalent comfort, which is a major reason stagnation is likely to endure. Underlying this endurance is the fact that zero or very slow economic growth in Japan still implies rising per capita income because Japan's population will soon begin to decline.

In the 1970s and 1980s, Japan was the economic wonder of the industrial world, recording the highest annual growth rate among all developed economies throughout this period. Its annual growth averaged above 4 percent, which transformed it into the world's second-largest economy. This remarkable record provoked a heated debate in policy and academic circles about explanations for the economic "miracle," as well as prognoses that Japan would either surpass the U.S. economy or at least would buy substantial parts of it!

During the 1990s and the first years of the twenty-first century, Japan's rapid growth was replaced by protracted economic stagnation, evoking hardly less wonderment, as well as a corre-

A slightly edited version was published in the *Los Angeles Times* on February 24, 2002, under the title "The Wages of Comfort."

sponding debate about explanations for this economic deterioration and its implications for Japan's future performance. This debate is tinged by irony because many commentators—in both policy and academic circles—who had previously offered convincing explanations for Japan's success, subsequently offered equally firm pronouncements about its more recent economic failures, having forgotten their categorical assertions about Japan's enduring success in the prior decades.

The Japanese miracle of the 1970s and 1980s was the result of several mutually reinforcing factors: high rates of savings and private (if "guided") capital formation; a skilled, vigorous, and growing labor force; a positive rate of productivity growth for both capital and labor; and an accommodating monetary policy that provided credit on favorable terms to aggressive, export-oriented industries and firms, especially in the automotive and electronic fields.

In combination, these factors overshadowed the accumulating inefficiencies resulting from a protected domestic market and an industrial policy in which government and the bureaucracy (notably, the Ministry of Finance and the Ministry of International Trade and Industry), rather than competitive markets, largely determined how and to what purposes resources were allocated.

Japan's stagnation in the 1990s and the first years of the twenty-first century has been driven by an equally potent set of forces, in large measure derived from the same factors contributing to the economic miracle of the 1970s and 1980s. These factors include

- An industrial system principally driven by considerations of economies of scale, increasing market share, and export growth, with profitability viewed as less important in determining resource allocations and the development of particular industries and firms.

- A banking system pervaded by huge nonperforming loans and weak balance sheets resulting from Japan's distorted industrial base and the credit misallocations associated with it.

- A regulatory system marked by the heavy hand of government and protectionism, limiting free entry and market access both within Japan and from potentially competitive firms outside, in the process stifling entrepreneurship and innovation. (Recent RAND work on economic openness found that Japan ranked far below the economies of both the United States and Germany, and about on a par with China and Korea, in its profusion of nontariff restrictions permeating the economy and impeding market access by foreign businesses.)

Reflecting as well as contributing to these negative drivers, the ratio of Japanese government investment to private investment nearly doubled between the 1980s and 1990s, and the absolute level of private investment declined by more than 12 percent in the same period. Correspondingly, the amount of new capital formation required per unit of added output more than doubled during the period, whereas the annual rise in productivity of both capital and labor plummeted, from just over 0.5 percent in the 1980s to a *negative* 2.1 percent in the 1990s.

To mitigate these circumstances, Japan's reforms have been somewhere between bland and modest. Those reforms have included loosened monetary policies with near-zero interest rates and government bailouts to the major banks to strengthen their fragile balance sheets and encourage new lending; increased levels of public spending, thereby expanding Japan's already large public debt, currently estimated between two and four times its GDP (the corresponding U.S. debt figure is less than half of GDP); and a modest degree of deregulation, allowing foreign investors to acquire Japanese assets in some fields.

Most observers, myself included, think these efforts are

inadequate. Without more drastic deregulation, Japan's near stagnation is likely to continue. RAND forecasts envisage Japan's annual growth in the first decade of the twenty-first century as likely
to hover between 0 and slightly above 1 percent annually.

Despite these trends, Japan is hardly in a crisis. It remains
wealthy, with per capita GDP among the highest in the world.
Sales of luxury consumer goods carrying the prestige labels of
Vuiton, Gucci, Hermes, and Courvoisier continue to be strong;
the standard of living of Japan's 127 million people is among the
highest in the industrial world; and its current account surplus
($117 billion in 2000) is the world's largest, as is its nearly $400
billion in foreign exchange reserves, almost twice those of second-
place China. Moreover, Japan's cities are generally among the
world's cleanest and safest. Public services are reliable and efficient by comparison with those elsewhere in the developed world.
(When one steps beyond the gate of an arriving flight in the
Tokyo or Osaka airports, within five seconds a noiseless and
speedy shuttle arrives to move one to another terminal for a con-
necting flight, a sharp contrast to what one found in U.S. airports
before September 11 and, more understandably, since then.) And,
even with low growth or zero growth in GDP, Japan's per capita
income will continue to rise because Japan's population will begin
to decline in the first decade of the twenty-first century; declining
population will, by 2010, have the effect of *raising* per capita income by nearly 1 percent in each subsequent five-year period,
even assuming that Japan's GDP remains unchanged!

Thus, stagnation in Japan is compatible with a high level of
consumer well-being and comfort, as it would not be in, say, the
United States or the European Union. This comfort level reduces
pressures for real structural reform to reinvigorate the Japanese
economy by pervasive deregulation, weeding out or consolidating
unprofitable firms and precarious banks through bankruptcies
and acquisitions, and creating a new business environment to en-

courage rather than discourage Japanese entrepreneurs, as well as foreign investors. Whether internal political pressure will be able to alter this "stagnation-with-comfort" scenario is doubtful. A more likely stimulus, if indeed any ensues, may be provided by China. If China's economic power or military power or both provide unequivocal evidence that China will eclipse Japan in the Asian regional context, the resulting shock in Japan may have consequences equivalent to those that occurred following the Meiji restoration in the late nineteenth century.

POSTAUDIT

The diagnosis of Japan's "miracle" growth of the 1970s and 1980s and its stagnation of the 1990s seems robust. That the economy now shows signs of improvement is plausibly and partly attributable to the wake-up call transmitted by China's resurgent growth. Other factors, too, have contributed to a brighter outlook, notably former prime minister Koizumi's taxation and other liberalizing reforms; MITI's (now renamed the Ministry of Economy, Trade and Industry) somewhat diminished influence; and the trimming of non-performing loans on banks' balance sheets.

9. Dealing with North Korea: Unilateralism, Bilateralism, or Multilateralism?

THE UNITED STATES has been roundly and frequently criticized for favoring multilateralism in the intermittent six-party talks aimed at reversing North Korea's pursuit of nuclear weapons. The critics favor a bilateral (which in practical terms means unilateral) approach in which the United States would engage directly in negotiations with Kim Jong-Il's regime; the four other parties (China, South Korea, Japan, and Russia) would be more passive.

In the critics' more "nuanced" formulation, the six-party label is acceptable as a facade, but progress toward ending North Korea's nuclear programs requires the United States to negotiate unilaterally with North Korea.

Ironically, these same critics have repeatedly and fervently castigated the U.S. stance in Iraq as forbiddingly unilateralist and professed a strong preference for multilateralism.

What is going on here? More precisely, what is the case for multilateralism rather than unilateralism in dealing with the tangled and dire North Korean threat?

A slightly edited version was published in the *Asian Wall Street Journal* on February 16, 2005, under the title "The Multilateral Path to Disarming North Korea."

This threat results from a North Korean stock of sufficient plutonium and highly enriched uranium to make (or to have already made) from six to eight nuclear weapons, together with a capability to deliver these weapons at distances of perhaps 5,500 miles. Still more worrisome is that North Korea might sell nuclear materials, technology, or disassembled weapons components to al-Qaeda or other terrorist organizations with ample funds; Kim Jong-Il's regime is so badly strapped for cash that its survival may depend on rapid access to substantial outside funding.

The case for emphasizing a multilateral approach to the North Korean threat rests on the premise that reaching the desired outcome of a nonnuclear North Korea should be shared among the five countries—China, Japan, South Korea, and Russia, in addition to the United States—because their separate and vital national interests are collectively involved.

China's interests in a nonnuclear North Korea focus on preventing nuclear proliferation elsewhere in Asia, specifically, in Japan, South Korea, and conceivably even Taiwan, that might be triggered by a North Korean nuclear threat. Moreover, the Shanghai Cooperation Organization (SCO), which China organized before the September 11, 2001, terrorist attacks on the United States, asserted a commitment by China, Russia, Kyrgyzstan, Kazakhstan, Tajikistan, and Uzbekistan to combat global terrorism. The SCO reflects China's concern lest North Korea be a channel through which nuclear materials and technology could leak to Uighur terrorists in China's own backyard of Sinkiang or elsewhere.

Japan's interests in a nonnuclear North Korea are no less vital than those of China or of the United States. Japan is keenly aware of the ingrained Korean resentment and hostility toward Japan. Were North Korea to acquire nuclear weapons conjoined with delivery capabilities that it has already demonstrated, Japanese policymakers might begin to doubt the adequacy of the U.S. protective nuclear umbrella. In these circumstances, responding to a likely clamor from the Japanese public, Japan might move toward acquiring its own nuclear deterrent, something that it already possesses ample technical and financial means to accomplish.

Although many in South Korea believe that a North Korean nuclear capability would not be directed against South Korea, the predominant view in the policy community is that a nuclear North Korea would profoundly disrupt Northeast Asia's security balance and thus imperil the region's stability on which South Korea's continued progress and economic growth depend.

Russia's stake in preventing a nuclear North Korea has been intensified by its plausible fear that nuclear devices might leak from North Korea to Chechnya's Islamist separatists, whose readiness to escalate their aggressive terrorism was shockingly demonstrated by their massacre of more than 300 children in Beslan on September 1, 2004. U.S. interests in preventing a nuclear North Korea are closely congruent with Russia's concern that a nuclear North Korea might become a channel for leakage of nuclear materials to global terrorism.

Although the individual national interests of the four other parties to the six-party talks—China, Japan, South Korea, and Russia—differ somewhat among the group, their individual and joint interests in reversing North Korean nuclear developments are at least equal to those of the United States.

Where a jointly favored, or "collective," benefit is sought by a group of countries, the crucial bottom line for their collaborative efforts is how the burden of securing this shared benefit should be shared. Multilateral management of the effort to halt North Korean nuclear development is essential. Whether and how much to use carrots and sticks, whether to apply force and penalties or combine them with the promise of beneficial transactions once all North Korea's nuclear programs have been terminated, requires collective, multilateral decisions.

For example, whether carrots in the form, say, of trade liberalization with and by North Korea or credit installments extended to North Korea and collateralized by claims on North Korean mineral resources, are options and decisions that must be arrived at multilaterally. Similarly, whether sticks in the form of inspection and monitoring of possible North Korean nuclear installations should be invoked, and whether the Proliferation Security Initiative should be strengthened and expanded to encompass surface and air surveillance and interdiction of suspected exports of nuclear materials and weapon system components, are other options and decisions that require collective judgment and choice.

In sum, securing a collective benefit—in this case, a nonnuclear North Korea—entails a collective burden and warrants multilateral leadership and multilateral enforcement.

POSTAUDIT

The arguments for and against multilateralism and unilateralism, respectively, as formulated in this article, remain intact two years after this was written. Indeed, North Korea's nuclear test on October 9, 2006, has reinforced the case for multilateralism.

---

10. Kim Jong-Il's Financial Bind

NORTH KOREA'S VOLATILE BEHAVIOR has confounded analysts for many years. Of late, the record has included adamant and protracted unwillingness to return to the six-party talks in Beijing followed by an expressed willingness to do so. In the interim, the DPRK's volatility included launching seven missile tests on July 5 (Pyongyang time but, notably, July 4 in the United States) and, on October 9, 2006, its celebratory announcement of a "successful" nuclear explosion.

Pyongyang has explained its behavior as a justifiable response to American hostility, to American unwillingness to engage in direct bilateral talks, and to North Korea's need for a nuclear deterrent against a potential attack from American forces.

Various pundits have conjectured that Kim Jong-Il's behavior is also driven by resentment over the shift of international attention toward Iran and away from North Korea and his desire to reverse this shift.

Although not dismissing these several explanations, a more

Published in the *Wall Street Journal Asia* on November 21, 2006, under the title "Tokyo's Leverage over Pyongyang."

important one probably lies in Kim Jong-Il's need for external sources of flexible funds to run North Korea's dynastic state. One indication of the explanation's importance is suggested by the North's October 30 agreement to return to the stalled six-party talks with the explicit understanding that the agenda will include the subject of financial sanctions, although without any concession thus far that the sanctions would be relaxed.

Whatever North Korea's motives, a central question that has bedeviled the on-again, off-again talks is, "Who has the economic or financial levers to induce Kim Jong-Il to reverse course, return to the six-party talks, halt the North's weapons of mass destruction programs and eventually terminate them in accord with the agreement reached in September 2005?"

The usual answer has been that China has the principal leverage through its continued benefactions (of fuel and food) to the North, whereas South Korea has somewhat less leverage. Yet both China and South Korea are reluctant to exercise this leverage for fear of the consequences: respectively, refugees flooding into China's Jilin and Liaoning provinces or artillery shelling of South Korea.

A key and typically neglected actor in this standard mise-en-scène is Japan, which may well have more financial leverage than is usually acknowledged and probably less compunction about using it than China or South Korea.

Japan's financial leverage derives from the substantial volume of hard-currency (dollar or yen) remittances to North Korea by Korean residents in Japan. Reliable data on the amount of these remittances are elusive, as well as spanning a wide range. The actual amounts, however, may well be even larger than the approximately $200 million represented by the excess of China's annual exports to North Korea (including fuel and food) above its imports from the North.

The principal source of these remittances from Japan is the

lucrative revenues accruing to Pachinko gaming parlors in Japan, one-quarter of which are owned by Koreans living in Japan. Although many of them do not favor the Kim regime, even those who don't may still have family members in the North and may believe or hope that the abject living conditions of their relatives will be at least slightly relieved by hard-currency transfers from Japan.

Pachinko, a favored and widespread pastime in Japan, generates gross revenues of more than 30 trillion yen annually, about $256 billion. Most of these revenues are absorbed by business expenses, taxation, and reinvestment, reducing the net income accruing to Korean owners by 75 percent or more. If as much as 2–3 percent of the remaining net income is transmitted to family and friends in the North through various channels—legal and illegal, by mail, by the limited tourism allowed by the North, by ship, by air, by routing through third and fourth countries—the resulting accruals to Kim Jong-Il may well amount to more than China's trade surplus with the DPRK.

Moreover, from Kim Jong-Il's perspective, these revenues have the added advantage of greater flexibility than the subventions provided by China in the form of specific commodities including food and fuel.

The critical importance of these revenues for the Kim dynastic regime can be inferred from the North's economic history and the regime's modus operandi.

In almost every year of North Korea's existence, it has incurred a balance of payments deficit (i.e., an excess of North Korean imports over its exports) of between $500 million and $1.5 billion. The same pattern occurred during the near half-century reign of Kim Il-Sung, the "Great Leader," until his demise in 1994, and during the twelve-year reign of his son, the "Dear Leader," Kim Jong-Il, since then.

During most of Kim Il-Sung's tenure, the principal source of funding for these deficits had been unrequited capital transfers from the Soviet Union. For most of Kim Jong-Il's reign, China and South Korea have been the major sources, along with growing reliance by North Korea on currency counterfeiting (of U.S. dollars) and remittances from the Korean diaspora in Japan.

Most of these revenues have accrued to the occupant of the dynastic Kim chair in Pyongyang. As did his father, so does Kim Jong-Il use this core of externally derived resources to provide the incentives and rewards that secure the loyalty and support of the key elites who manage the system: the generals in the Korean People's Army; the technocrats who direct the economy's industries, including its defense industry; and the top echelons of the Korean Workers Party. Any sign of weakened loyalty or diminished support within these elites results in withdrawal of rewards and their replacement by more severe penalties. Compliant behavior enables the system to survive.

Viewed in this light, several actions by the United States, China, and Japan during the past several months may appear to Kim Jong-Il as constituting a fundamental threat to the regime's survival. Those actions include the U.S. Treasury Department's designation of Macau's Delta Asia Bank as a primary vehicle for money laundering in Asia and specifically as a repository for North Korean accounts derived from counterfeiting of U.S. currency and from other illicit practices. With the cooperation of China, this designation led to the closing of the Delta Asia Bank and the freezing of several other overseas North Korean accounts.

Another worry signaled by Japan, and probably more likely to materialize under the administration of its new prime minister, Shinzo Abe, than his predecessor, Junichiro Koizumi, involves careful monitoring and prospective curtailment of remittances by North Korean residents in Japan of the net earnings from the lucrative Pachinko casinos, referred to above.

China's influence was probably decisive in inducing North

Korea to announce its willingness to return to the six-party talks. It is likely that Japan's influence will be crucial if the talks are to succeed in meeting their salient objectives.

In the long run, reversing and terminating Pyongyang's nuclear program requires addressing as central issues the financial and operational characteristics of the North Korean system, not just the issues of political and security threats by or to North Korea, which thus far have been the principal focus of attention. For the system to survive, it must change. It must be modernized so it can gain access to the financial support that normal integration into the world economy will bring through trade, capital transactions, and tourism and forgo its endeavors to acquire such funding through illicit and hazardous means.

POSTAUDIT

Japan's leverage is both more important than is usually acknowledged and too often neglected in discussions of and with North Korea.

PART THREE

Other Regions

11. Europe's Unilateralism May Have a Brighter Side

WHEN AMERICA'S EUROPEAN ALLIES complain about the putative unilateralism of the United States, it's hardly news. But rarely, if ever, does the United States return the complaint. It isn't entirely clear whether this asymmetry is because Americans are less aware of Europe's unilateralist proclivities or simply pay less attention to them.

A case in point is the European Union's recent unilateral abandonment of the European Security and Defense Policy (ESDP) and its designated instrument, the European Rapid Reaction Force (ERRF). Although largely ignored in the press, this action follows nearly ten years of fulsome rhetoric, innumerable conferences, white papers, communiqués, and negotiations intended to convert ESDP from a concept into a reality. The underlying concept was to provide a collective security capability for the EU that would support and effectuate its emergent foreign and security policies.

The initial U.S. reaction to ESDP was lukewarm, if not neg-

A slightly edited version was published in the *Wall Street Journal Europe*, on May 17, 2002, under the title "Europeans Are Unilateralists Too."

ative, because of concern that an autonomous EU security establishment would weaken and perhaps sunder the NATO alliance. This concern was heightened by the fact that ESDP was being promoted at about the same time as an initiative was getting under way within NATO to upgrade and modernize the military capabilities of the alliance's European members. Hence, it was feared by the Americans that ESDP might distract attention and subtract resources from this defense capabilities initiative within NATO.

Countering these concerns, there was within U.S. policy circles a favorable view of ESDP that, although initially a minority opinion, had become the predominant view by 2001, at the end of William Cohen's tenure as secretary of defense. The central premise of this view was that, in light of the Balkan experience, European military capabilities and military technology were so badly lagging that perhaps ESDP could play a valuable role in upgrading them. Moreover, as the ESDP discussions with the Americans as well as within the EU evolved, the capabilities envisaged for the ERRF increasingly suggested that they could have a complementary rather than conflicting relationship to U.S. and NATO forces. Specifically, ERRF was to be a 60,000-person force developed from existing European military units or by forming new ones. According to the "Headline Goals" of ESDP, the ERRF would be *interoperable* with U.S. forces as well as rapidly deployable and equipped with advanced command-and-control and other high-tech military systems reflecting the so-called revolution in military affairs.

As a result, U.S. concerns about ESDP's possible adverse effects on NATO were replaced by the view that ESDP might be useful as a potential contributor to more equitable burden sharing by the EU in international peacemaking and hence beneficial to U.S. global security interests.

Although this altered perspective preceded the attacks of September 11, there were reasonable grounds in its wake to hope that an upgraded, high-tech, flexible, and interoperable EU force could, on balance, also be a valuable asset in the global war on terrorism. For example, if the EU force were a reality rather than a rhetorical figment, it could play a major role in the International Security Assistance Force in Afghanistan, thereby contributing to its stability and reconstruction, to which the EU has pledged its support no less than has the United States. Interoperability between the ERRF and U.S. special and regular forces engaged in search and destroy operations against remaining al-Qaeda and Taliban forces could thus be mutually advantageous.

At this point, enter European unilateralism!

As the discussion of ESDP has evolved over the past decade, much of the agenda dealt with concepts, doctrine, and policies, with little concrete attention devoted to the costs that the ERRF would entail were it to be seriously pursued. Preliminary analysis at RAND has placed the military investment costs (i.e., development and procurement) of the ERRF in a conservative range estimated between $24 billion and $56 billion—about twice that of current annual military investment outlays in the four major EU countries—Germany, France, Britain, and Italy.

As the time approached to face up to the need for boosting defense outlays—especially in light of 9/11—the EU has quietly and unilaterally shelved ESDP! With the exception of the United Kingdom, the EU has placed ESDP in a limbo from which it is unlikely ever to emerge.

Yet there may be some partly redemptive aspects to this exercise of European unilateralism. Maybe our European allies will be less disposed to complain in the future about what they regard as instances of U.S. unilateralism if they are reminded of their own. A possible rebuttal by the EU that its abandonment of ESDP is strictly an internal matter, hence not properly unilateralist, is a flawed argument. Abandoning ESDP has repercussions—what economists call *externalities*—that affect the interests of the United States, Turkey, and others, but consultations with these affected parties were not held before ESDP was unilaterally jettisoned.

Finally, perhaps those in the U.S. policy community who were initially skeptical that ESDP and the ERRF would complement rather than conflict with NATO as well as with U.S. policies may have been right all along. The unilateral abandonment of ESDP effectively removes this concern.

POSTAUDIT

Comparing this piece with chapter 9 on America's frequent disposition toward multilateralism, one can infer that Europe's disposition toward unilateral action exceeds that of the United States, despite conventional wisdom to the contrary!

12. Absent Weapons
Don't Imply
Faulty Intelligence

THE U.S. DECISION TO LAUNCH military action against Iraq was heavily influenced by a belief that Iraq possessed weapons of mass destruction (WMD) that, if not destroyed, could, directly or indirectly, and sooner or later, threaten the security of the United States. Thus far, the weapons have not been found, although they may be in the future. On the other hand, they may not be.

In light of this possibility, the media, Congress, and the intelligence community itself have begun to focus on whether the absence of WMD in Iraq would imply that the intelligence on which the prior belief was based was either flawed or deliberately slanted? Many respondents to this question—especially, but not only, those who had originally opposed the war in Iraq—would answer it affirmatively.

They would be wrong: an unexpected outcome from an inescapably probabilistic estimate does not signify that the estimate was flawed or slanted! Intelligence estimates in general, as well as in the specific instance of WMD in Iraq, are inherently and

A slightly edited version was published in the *Wall Street Journal Europe* on July 18–20, 2003, under the title ". . . But the Decision for War Was Still Right."

inescapably uncertain, which is to say that they are probabilistic. Estimates made about something to be found or experienced in the future can at most only lead to a conclusion that there is a probability of some conjectured magnitude that a specified outcome will be realized.

Colin Powell's strong presentation to the U.N. Security Council on February 5 cited cell phone intercepts, satellite imagery, and other information sources to support the belief that Iraq possessed WMD. Yet, no matter how compelling the evidence, the inference from it was inescapably probabilistic. Yesterday's evidence, no matter how abundant and compelling, can only yield an estimate that there's a high probability—never a certainty—of what will be found tomorrow. Tangible evidence compiled yesterday, let alone strong circumstantial clues, can only warrant an inference that the probability of one particular outcome, in this case Iraq's possession of WMD, is higher than that of another, namely, the probability of nonpossession.

If, despite these relative probabilities, WMD are not found, this outcome does not imply that the prior estimate was wrong. The prior estimate may have been accurate even given the unexpected outcome, which may be attributable not only to the absence of WMD but also to the possibility that weapons possessed by Iraq prior to March 19 were subsequently destroyed, moved to another country, or, in the case of chemical and biological weapons, decomposed into relatively inconspicuous and innocuous precursor elements or agents. So an unexpected outcome may ensue notwithstanding the accuracy of a prior forecast that its occurrence was unlikely.

This line of reasoning raises two central questions that have been largely ignored in the debate about the elusive or nonexisting WMD in Iraq. The first is how to make intelligence estimates and estimators accountable. Unexpected outcomes can occur notwithstanding the accuracy of prior estimates that such outcomes are unlikely. But unexpected outcomes may also ensue because the estimates of their likelihood were faulty. How can intelligence users, let alone the general public, know whether the occurrence of an unexpected outcome resulted from the complexity of circumstances and the range of uncertainty associated with them or from the incompetence of the estimators?

The laws of probability suggest an answer. If an unexpected outcome ensues once or twice, it may not be surprising or conclusive: for example, if there were something like a five-to-one probability that Iraq had WMD, but in fact none is found, this would hardly provide grounds for faulting the estimate. If, however, for several unrelated estimates—for example, the probability of North Korea's development of nuclear weapons and delivery capabilities—unexpected outcomes recur, then the likelihood that the estimators and the estimation process are broken and need repair rises exponentially.

The second question is whether the war in Iraq should have been delayed until even more conclusive evidence of Iraq's possession of WMD had been acquired or, to the contrary, some compelling evidence of Iraq's nonpossession of WMD was brought to light.

The answer requires recognizing two different types of error that decision makers confront, either explicitly or implicitly. One type may result if the decision maker supposes that a particular outcome will materialize—say, that Iraq has (or did have) WMD—but, despite the high probability associated with this outcome, it turns out that this supposition is wrong, that is, Iraq really does (or did) not have WMD. The second type of error is the reverse: if the decision maker supposes that a different outcome will materialize—for example, Iraq doesn't (or didn't) have WMD—but instead it turns out that this supposition is wrong, namely, that Iraq really does (or did) have WMD.

The decision maker's dilemma is to choose which of the two

possible errors is less hazardous to accept or, more important, to avoid. The Bush administration clearly decided that the second type of error was of such grave concern for the security interests of the United States that the risk of making this error had to be avoided.

Whether one agrees with this decision (which I do), or disagrees with it, there's no question that in the final analysis it is precisely the sort of judgment that the American public pays the president to make.

POSTAUDIT

This primer on some elements of probability theory and the dilemma facing decision makers remains as valid now and prospectively as it was then.

---

13. Resolving the UN Dilemma

DEPENDING ON WHOM YOU TALK TO, the UN is either an obstacle to more effective security and reconstruction efforts in Iraq or an opportunity to advance precisely these goals.

Adherents of the view that the UN is an obstacle cite the UN's propensity for dilatory political wrangling, semantic hairsplitting, and diplomatic horse-trading—all much in evidence in the two months required for the United States to obtain Security Council approval on October 16 of an artfully worded resolution endorsing an accelerated process of security, reconstruction, and movement toward a sovereign Iraqi state. Like other UN endeavors, this one involved U.S. negotiations not only with the 4 other veto-wielding permanent Security Council members, but also with the 10 rotating members who, in turn, engaged in discussions with others of the remaining 176 members of the General Assembly.

Adherents of the view that the UN provides a significant and valuable opportunity present a very different perspective. They argue that the Security Council process is essential as both in-

A slightly edited version was published in the *International Herald Tribune* on November 13, 2003, under the title "Pick the UN's Best for a Wider Iraq Role."

ducement and political cover if several countries are to be politically enabled to provide military and paramilitary forces and
other assistance in Iraq. Some of those countries—including India,
South Korea, Bangladesh, and perhaps Russia and Indonesia—
disagreed with the coalition's original decision to invade Iraq in
March and thus would need the endorsement of a Security Council resolution to change course now. So, the argument goes, the
Security Council process is an opportunity to obtain the participation and assistance that we seek.

In the U.S. policy community, protagonists of the obstacle
view are concentrated in the Pentagon, whereas adherents to the
opportunity view populate the State Department.

In any event, there may be a way to resolve this dilemma—a
way that can reinforce and add muscle to the Security Council
resolution. This alternative lies in directly expanding the role of
a select few of the UN's specialized agencies to pursue in Iraq the
humanitarian and reconstruction activities in which they are com-
petent and experienced. This approach not only complements
the UN resolution of October 16 but also constitutes a more effective means of inducing other countries to provide military and
paramilitary forces to strengthen security in Iraq.

The UN consists of nearly two dozen specialized agencies,
some of which have highly creditable track records for providing effective as well as efficient services, despite the fact that
others are cumbersome, cost-ineffective bureaucracies. The high-
performance agencies include the World Health Organization,
the Food and Agricultural Organization, the UN International
Children's Emergency Fund, the UN Development Program, the
UN Industrial Development Organization, and the International
Telecommunications Union.

Now suppose the Coalition Provisional Authority and Iraq's
Governing Council, together with such other financially able governments as those of Japan, Britain, the Netherlands, Denmark,

Poland, perhaps South Korea, China, and others, proposed to UN secretary-general Kofi Annan to augment significantly the core budgets of these agencies—say, by 20 percent—to support resumption and expansion of their reconstruction efforts in Iraq: for example, by children's vaccination and nutrition programs, technical assistance in agriculture and water supply, rehabilitation and repair of electricity and telecommunication systems, and training telecom technicians.

The annual budgets of the six UN agencies referred to above amount to approximately $2.6 billion. So, shared among the financially able donors, the annual costs of the proposed 20 percent increased UN effort would be about $500 million—whose U.S. share would fit within, rather than add to, the $18.3 billion for Iraq's reconstruction that the Bush administration has obtained from Congress.

In light of the unanimous and permissive resolution 1511, it is likely that the secretary-general would be inclined to accept this proposal, both because it would advance reconstruction in Iraq and because it would ease the UN's budgetary woes—a matter that Annan frequently bemoans, both inside and outside UN corridors. In the wake of the tragic August 19, 2003, bombing of the UN compound in Baghdad, Annan's acceptance would no doubt be conditional on assurance of enhanced security for UN personnel.

Anticipation of such a substantial expansion of the UN presence in Iraq would constitute a more powerful de facto UN mandate than does resolution 1511 alone, thereby facilitating the provision by certain key countries of military and paramilitary forces to enhance security on the ground. Providing these forces would undergird an expanded UN role in Iraq's reconstruction, as well as being vindicated by that expanded role. In effect, the expanded UN role in Iraq's reconstruction would constitute a strong political rationale and justification for providing military and paramilitary forces, as well.

Acceptance of the proposal would, of course, also carry with it retention by the UN of its authority and responsibility to ensure that the expanded role of the selected UN agencies was exercised in full conformity with the UN's established humanitarian and nation-building missions.

Thus, the expanded UN activities would palpably reinforce the case for additional forces to enhance security for the conduct of these activities.

The result would be a compelling synergy. Expansion of the UN role in Iraq's reconstruction would encourage contributions of military and police forces to enhance security in Iraq, and the improved security would contribute to a more effective UN role in Iraq's reconstruction.

POSTAUDIT

The basic idea of explicitly linking part of the U.S. (and other countries') financial contributions to the relatively effective and high-performing specialized agencies of the UN is appropriately analogous to the notion of conditionality in foreign aid. That the idea would be distinctly unwelcome in the UN Secretariat was amply demonstrated in a seminar I gave to several dozen senior UN officials in New York in 2003 shortly before this was published. I think this cool reception might have been a good and sufficient reason for pursuing the idea further at the time.

14. What if
   Iraq Had
   Not Been
   Invaded?

NEWS ABOUT IRAQ during the past two months has ranged from not good to extremely bad, with illustrative events including the Abu Ghraib abominations, mounting evidence of civil disorder, and sustained military and civilian casualties.

Forecasts drawing from this news have envisaged continued deterioration, reflected in repetitive use of the term *quagmire* resurrected from the Vietnam era.

Although I admit that the Iraqi glass currently appears less than half full, I want to focus on a few items of good news that have been neglected by the media and in most public discussion. These items are not the ones that have from time to time been reported on—such as progress in the reconstruction part of Operation Iraqi Freedom, for example, schools and hospitals rebuilt and back in operation, oil production above preinvasion levels, and so on.

Presented as a dinner talk in June 2004 to a group of financial executives, but never published.

The things I'll mention briefly fall into two categories:

First, indistinct but growing signs that Iraq's disparate groups and their leaders may be coalescing, or "consensualizing," to at least the extent that *maybe*—just maybe—they'll be able to give reality to the abstract notion of exercising sovereignty post-June 30.

Second, what if we hadn't invaded Iraq on March 19, 2003; what would the situation have been and now be in and around Iraq? This is something critics of the war never consider. I opine that the situation in Iraq currently would be decidedly worse than it now is—that is to say, worse for the United States and, as well, worse for the world.

To start with the first category:

Several recent and ongoing circumstances constitute what may be emerging signs of a tenably sovereign Iraq after June 30. These circumstances include the following:

1. The four-way agreement negotiated among Muktada al Sadr, the Grand Ayatollah Sistani and the city fathers and Shia clerics, the Fifth U.S. Marine Brigade, and the Iraq Governing Coalition (IGC), calling for al Sadr and his Mahdi army to evacuate police stations, mosques, and other city buildings in Falluja and Najaf and lay down their arms and for the marines to withdraw to the city outskirts.

2. The agreements (negotiated among many more than four sides) that the interim "sovereign" Iraqi government will have at its head a Shiite prime minister, Ayad Allawi; a Sunni president (either Pachachi or al Ghazi); and two vice presidents—one a Kurd and the other a Shiite.

3. Frankly, I don't profess to understand all the ins and outs of these negotiations—either those relating to Falluja and Najaf or those relating to the interim "sovereign" Iraqi government—but a couple of things about them seem clear and im-

portant: first, all sides seem to have given some things up, as well as gotten some things they wanted; second, the Iraqis—on the IGC and the clerics outside of it—seem to have stood up quite vociferously both to Brahimi (Kofi's guy), and to Bremer and Blackwill on the CPA and U.S. side, rejecting what the latter "3-B's" separately or jointly preferred. I think both of these are indications of what I referred to as "consensualizing," and are at least mildly encouraging signs of a tenable post–June 30 "sovereign" Iraq.

Let me turn next to the "what if?" category. Suppose the United States and its coalition partners hadn't invaded Iraq, what would the situation there now be? Would we—that is, the United States—be in a better or worse position? And what about the world at large?

Of course, we don't know: a counterfactual situation is not scrutable. But consider the following as a plausible—in my opinion, highly probable—counterfactual scenario:

1. The 60,000–70,000 U.S. forces in Kuwait, Qatar, Saudi Arabia, and adjoining Arab states in the preinvasion period would for logistic and other reasons have returned to their U.S. or other normal bases.

2. Hans Blix and the UN inspectors would have returned to Iraq for another couple of months, have found nothing, and then, like Robert Frost's fog, have silently faded away.

3. The UN sanctions imposed on Iraq would have been ended at the behest of the French and the Russians, or, if token sanctions were maintained, they would have been severely attenuated. Concomitantly, the oil-for-food-and-medicines program would have been terminated and, incidentally, the oil-for-food UN scandal that Paul Volker and associates are ostensibly investigating would have been forever buried.

4. Saddam not only would still be in power but would now have both enormously enhanced resources to pursue WMD development discreetly but aggressively, probably with ample assistance from A.Q. Khan and Kim Jong-Il.

5. Finally, secular Saddam, now endowed with increased financial resources, would have forged indirect financial and perhaps strategic and operational cooperation with Osama, Zarkawi, and al-Qaeda's other top echelons.

Bottom line: Homeland security in the United States as well as the global security environment would be much more severely imperiled than it currently is. QED: The United States and the world are better off for having invaded Iraq than they would have been had not this "preemptive" action been undertaken!!

POSTAUDIT

These remarks were originally given at a corporate dinner, fifteen months after U.S. and coalition forces invaded Iraq. Retrospectively, the analysis summarized in the essay still seems sound, although the conclusion drawn from it is less convincing.

15. How Sunni Capitalism Can Trump Sunni Insurgency

PRIVATIZING IRAQ's lucrative oil assets and vesting every Iraqi citizen with an equal number of shares can provide tangible incentives for every Iraqi—including Sunnis, who are the insurgency's core supporters—to view security and commerce as a better path to follow than insurgency and violence. Every Iraqi would own a piece of Iraq, providing Iraq's 28 million citizens with a prospective increase in per capita annual income of about $5,800, a substantial boost.

This is unlikely to persuade the hard-core, committed al-Qaeda/Zarqawi terrorists to change course. But turning all Iraqis into stockholders in the nation's oil wealth can win over the support of the bulk of the Sunni population that now backs the insurgency by providing foot soldiers, intelligence, cover, safe houses, or simply passive acceptance.

Iraq's oil reserves, estimated at 115 billion barrels (bbl), are the world's third largest, after Saudi Arabia and Iran (263 bbl and 133 bbl, respectively). The location of these reserves within the

A slightly edited version was published in the *Wall Street Journal* on November 23, 2005, under the title "Shareholders Don't Shoot Each Other."

ethnically divided federal Iraqi state, however, presents a problem. About 80 percent of the oil is located in southern Iraq, where
the Shia who constitute 60 percent of Iraq's population predominate; about 15–18 percent of the oil is in northern Iraq, where
the Kurds, who constitute 20 percent of the population, are concentrated. The problem is that less than 5 percent of Iraq's lucrative oil reserves are located in the three provinces in central
Iraq—Al-Anbar, Nineveh, and Salahuddin—where most of the 20
percent of the Iraqi population that is Sunni lives.

In a federal, democratic Iraq whose majority population is
Shia and whose most lucrative assets are located in areas where
Shia and Kurds predominate, it is not surprising that Sunnis have
a dim view of their future. Their future appears even gloomier
when benchmarked against the twenty-five years of Saddam's rule
in which Sunnis had it all: privilege, status, as well as the oil assets,
regardless of their geographic location.

A readily though perhaps not easily available financial innovation can go a long way toward redressing this portentous Sunni
outlook.

At present Iraq's oil assets are a government monopoly. Privatizing these assets and giving every Iraqi an equal share in their
ownership can be accomplished by turning over the assets to private companies—perhaps two companies in the South and one
each in North and Central Iraq—and vesting all Iraqi citizens with
equal shareholdings in each company, for example, 5 shares or
10 shares to each Iraqi in each company. Shares could be traded
at market-determined prices, but trading would be limited to Iraqis, at least for an initial period of, say, five to ten years, after
which the market might be opened to foreign participation.

In effect, the new stock issuance would be an exclusive public
offering (EPO), issued gratis to Iraqis on an equal per capita basis.
Company management would be responsible to shareholders in
accord with the guidelines of sound corporate governance. Cor-

porate earnings and dividends achieved by management for the benefit of shareholders would affect share prices as well as management tenure and compensation. Assuming full disclosure and certification of financial reports to shareholders and independent corporate directors, laggard management performance would result in management replacement. Government would derive revenues by taxing corporate and shareholder income.

What would that be worth to Iraqis? Assume that oil reserves in the ground are valued at $20 a barrel, and assume further that 30 percent of the total asset value is mortgaged and absorbed up front to finance new and replacement infrastructure investment in the newly formed companies. The remaining book value for each Iraqi's total share holdings is estimated at about $58,000. A conservative ratio of return to net asset value of, say, 10 percent would yield for each Iraqi citizen an annual income of $5,800. For a Sunni family of four this would represent a large increment in its annual income.

Sunnis would not be confined to the 20 percent of the shares they'd receive from the initial EPO in accord with their proportionate size in the Iraqi population. They could trade up and acquire additional shares, as, of course, could other ethnic groups of Iraqi citizens, depending on their financial capabilities, business acumen, and career aspirations.

The numbers suggest an enormous opportunity for family betterment through schooling, health services, housing, and community improvement. Although this brighter future would not turn the committed jihadists, it could change the environment in

which they operate by attracting the majority of less committed
or uncommitted Sunnis.

POSTAUDIT

Before and after writing this proposal I have repeatedly
thought that a missing ingredient in Iraq strategy has been
a determined and high-priority effort to elicit mutual self-
interested cooperation among the ethnic communities in
conflict. Iraq's huge oil resources provide the most important vehicle for doing this. Among the various proposals for
addressing this matter, the one described in this essay seems
to me the best. Despite acknowledgment of the idea by U.S.
policy officialdom, no evidence of implementation efforts
has ensued.

16. Signs of Regress and Progress in Russia's Economy

WHEN ASKED MORE THAN sixty-five years ago for his opinion about the Soviet Union, Winston Churchill observed: "I cannot forecast . . . the action of Russia. It is a riddle wrapped in a mystery inside an enigma."

Since the collapse of the Soviet Union in 1990 and the ensuing Russian administrations of Boris Yeltsin and Vladimir Putin, much of the previous riddle has been resolved as a result of Russia's opening to international trade, investment, and tourism; to the media and the Internet; and to the publication of voluminous (if not always completely reliable) data on the Russian economy and society. Nevertheless, despite Russia's inclusion in the G-8 group of supposedly "advanced industrialized democracies," much of Russia's current situation and future prospects can still appropriately be characterized as "a mystery inside an enigma."

Of the numerous economies often termed to be transitional, Russia's—with a GDP of about one-fifth that of China but a per

Published in the *Japan Times* on January 11, 2007, under the title "Russia's Progress and Regress."

capita product twice that of China—is the second largest. Exactly where the Russian economy fits in the market-oriented gamut of transitioning economies is, however, not yet clear: between, say, Belarus, Uzbekistan, and Vietnam at one end, and the Balkan and Central European States and China at the other end? Also unclear is the pace of the Russian economy's transition and whether it is headed forward, toward market-oriented, decentralized resource allocation; or backward, toward centralized, state-controlled allocation; or oscillating between these two.

Yegor Gaidar, a distinguished economist and former Russian prime minister, has conjectured that Russia's full transition to a market-based economy is likely to take about seventy-five years because of the long "duration of the Socialist period and the distortions connected with it." Nonetheless, Russia has been recognized by the United States and the European Union as a "market economy," a status that ostensibly makes it less likely to have other market economies impose "anti-dumping" or other protectionist measures on its exports. That this status has been accorded to Russia as much for political as economic reasons is suggested by the fact that Russia is not yet a member of the World Trade Organization.

A vehement debate is currently under way within Russia concerning the direction of Russia's economic transition. The debate reflects the sharply different emphasis placed by the two sides on either the "good news" (favoring market-oriented changes) or the "bad news" (heading in the reverse direction). The debate also highlights disagreements about the reliability of certain official data—notably, whether the striking evidence of private-sector growth portrayed by official statistics is credible. The bad news side of the debate contends that the level of state ownership, state production, and state employment prevailing in the Russian economy is at least as large in 2006 as it was before the arrest in 2002 of Yukos's chief executive, Mikhail Khodorkovsky. In sharp contrast is the view of the good-news advocates, who aver that the official data on private-sector growth actually *understate* the pace and magnitude of Russia's transition toward private ownership and market-oriented resource allocation. These advocates contend that the understatement results from efforts by private businesses to avoid or reduce their tax liabilities by not registering or by underreporting the scale of their business activities.

In fact, Russia's economic performance since 1991 has been relatively favorable: its real GDP growth has been more than twice the unweighted average of the other G-8 members (Japan, Germany, France, Canada, Italy, the United Kingdom, and the United States). During President Putin's tenure since 2000, Russia's annual GDP growth has been 6 percent. Foreign debt has been reduced from 50 percent of GDP to less than 30 percent, and Russia's $3.3 billion debt to the International Monetary Fund was repaid ahead of schedule in 2005; of the $40 billion owed to its creditors in the Paris Club, Russia paid $15 billion ahead of schedule. During this period, Russia's foreign exchange reserves have more than tripled, to more than $250 billion.

Thus, although the good economic news is ample, there are also significant indicators of bad news. Inflation continues to hover around 10 percent, and capital flight—an indicator of weakened confidence in the Russian economy among holders of ruble assets—was more than $9 billion in 2004 and increased above that rate in 2005.

Concerning the good economic news and Russia's generally favorable economic performance, how much of it should properly be attributed to higher oil and natural gas prices (hence, to factors not under Russia's control), and how much should be attributed to economic reform (hence, subject to greater influence by domestic Russian policies)?

Empirical work at the RAND Corporation clearly reflects the Russian economy's heavy dependence on fossil fuels: oil and natural gas prices explain between one-third and two-fifths of Russian economic growth over the period from 1993 through 2005. Oil and gas production has accounted for between 16 and 20 percent of Russia's GDP and between 44 and 55 percent of Russia's total export revenues since 2004. The buildup of Russian foreign exchange reserves mentioned earlier is a further illustration of this dependence.

Besides this dependence on oil and gas prices and revenues (notably, global oil prices have fallen by 20 percent from their July 2000 highs), several other indicators suggest that economic reform has also contributed to the economy's good news. In the past decade, the number of privately owned enterprises more than doubled, rising to nearly 80 percent of all enterprises, whereas state-owned enterprises during this period shrank from 14 percent to less than 4 percent of all enterprises. Perhaps of greater significance, the volume of employment in private enterprises grew by 41 percent, whereas that in state enterprises declined by 15 percent. The expansion of private enterprise that occurred—especially of medium-size and small-scale enterprises—covers a wide range of both higher- and lower-technology goods and services, including computer and information technology, financial services, engineering and construction, spare parts manufacturing, and repair and maintenance services. Moreover, as suggested earlier, these data probably understate the actual growth of the private sector: privately owned enterprises—particularly those with fifty or fewer employees—are more likely to avoid their inclusion in the official data, choosing instead to pay a "protection" price to avoid taxes and to escape from the myriad regulatory constraints that might be imposed were they registered in the official data.

A final good news indicator that reflects both external (oil and gas prices) and internal (economic reform) influences is the recent boosting by the major securities' rating agencies of Russia's sovereign debt status from junk to investment-grade. These rating enhancements are significant because they lower the cost to Russia of access to global capital markets and also represent at least a modest expression of confidence in the Russian economy's prospects.

In sum, where the Russian economy is heading—toward decentralized resource allocation by competitive markets or backward toward decision making by the state and its bureaucracies, toward greater reliance on private, market-driven enterprise or back to state enterprise and state regulation—remains highly uncertain. No less uncertain is what these economic puzzles imply with respect to Russia's role and behavior in the international arena.

Although the context has changed drastically, Winston Churchill's insight in 1939 remains strikingly accurate today!

POSTAUDIT

This piece was written too recently to claim much prescience. Fueled by high oil and gas prices, the Russian economy continues its strong performance; the uncertainties and ambiguities remain as discussed in this essay.

PART FOUR

The Global View

17. The Case
for Selective
Unilateralism

SOME CRITICS OF U.S. FOREIGN POLICY spend as much time complaining about its unilateral style as about its substance. To be sure, the line between style and substance is blurred. Branding U.S. policy as unilateral may simply be a way of discrediting, rather than contesting, its substance. U.S. policy and its architects are said by the critics to shun consultation with others, including allies, to ignore divergent opinions, and, when a course of action is decided on, to launch it unilaterally as a fait accompli.

That this package of beliefs is remote from reality doesn't prevent its prevalence. Contrary to it and the accompanying rhetoric, U.S. foreign policies typically involve extensive consultation with other countries, as well as receptivity to divergent views. Although "receptivity" implies openness to divergent views, it doesn't signify pliant readiness to trade off putative U.S. national interests—sometimes including major domestic interests—to achieve a wider international consensus.

At this point in the argument, the issue begins to move from criticism of the style of U.S. policies to their substance. To dissect the miscast unilateralist critique, consider three of the most salient policy issues that critics have highlighted and reiterated as examples of U.S. unilateralism: the Kyoto Treaty on emissions controls and global warming; missile defense and its link to the demise of the Antiballistic Missile (ABM) Treaty of 1972; and foreign aid as grants rather than loans.

- Endorsement of the Kyoto Protocol by the Clinton adminis- tration was openly and repeatedly disavowed by the Bush team both during the 2000 campaign and afterward. More- over, the several reasons prompting disavowal were discussed and explained multilaterally, repetitively, and extensively, in- cluding that compliance would impose added burdens on a U.S. economy already showing signs of weakness. Another reason was the treaty's technically flawed focus on *gross* emis- sions of CO_2 rather than *net* emissions, which would allow for absorption of CO_2 by forests and grasslands. Focusing on the proper indicator of *net* emissions would reduce U.S. emissions to very low levels for this alleged source of global warming, whatever the scientific basis for the allegations. A third reason for disavowal was the Senate's earlier passage, by an over- whelming margin, of a resolution that repudiated the proto- col—thereby decisively indicating that approval of the treaty wasn't in the cards. So, despite all the international criticism of the U.S. "unilateral disavowal of Kyoto," this outcome had been multilaterally discussed and foreshadowed. It was em- phatically not arrived at unilaterally.

- Turning to missile defense and the demise of the ABM Treaty, admittedly many concerns remain about missile de- fense that warrant further analysis and assessment. But there should be no question about the abundance, openness, and multilateralism of the debate. Before the U.S. decision to pro- ceed aggressively with missile defense, and to withdraw from the treaty as provided for in the treaty itself, the United States held innumerable meetings and discussions on both subjects with NATO allies, Russia, China, and Japan. Affixing a "unilateral" label to this process or its outcome is contrary to the facts. The distinctly multilateral character of the debate was certified by the formal Treaty of Moscow, signed by Presidents Bush and Putin on May 24, 2002, which combined sharp reductions in nuclear warheads (from 5,000–6,500 on each side to between 1,700 and 2,200 by 2012), together with the possibility of collaboration between the signatories to accelerate development, testing, and deployment of thin national missile defense systems.

- A third instance of supposed U.S. unilateralism has been the administration's contention that, when foreign aid is provided to poor countries, it should be in the form of grants rather than loans, contrary to the prevailing practice. The logic of this position, which has been presented and discussed in countless international forums, consists of four propositions: first, that foreign aid to poor countries should be conditioned on their improved performance; second, that this improvement should be their ticket for access to the global capital markets to replace foreign aid; third, that a severe and mounting impediment to such access results from the accumulation by these countries of debt owed for foreign aid received by them bilaterally and from the World Bank, the International Monetary Fund, and the numerous regional development banks; finally, that the acute difficulty many less-developed countries experience in servicing their accumulated debt often imposes increasingly severe interest charges on further borrowing, thereby indefinitely deferring their access to global capital markets. Although the economic logic is compelling, and has been presented in many multilateral conferences among policymakers and financial experts, thus far it has not elicited multilateral acceptance.

These examples are typical. Other prominent ones cited by unilateralist critics include the frequently expressed U.S. intention to remove Saddam Hussein and the U.S. decision to oppose the new United Nations International Criminal Court and to preclude it from having any jurisdiction over U.S. military forces engaged in peacekeeping activities—a stance the UN has reluctantly accepted. These cases exhibit a similar pattern: extensive and intensive U.S. consultation and interaction with other countries, combined with ample readiness to consider divergent views and to delay action while reaffirming U.S. concerns and interests.

At day's end, the ace-in-the-hole argument adduced by critics of U.S. unilateralism is pragmatic and opportunistic, quite apart from issues of style or substance. The United States, they contend, should be more willing to compromise on substance and on U.S. national interests because it would make allies and friends more disposed toward cooperation and burden-sharing when we need them in the future. Ironically, the war on terrorism provides a strong counterargument. After September 11, 2001, the U.S. war against terrorism in Afghanistan and globally was initiated unilaterally and, in the process, galvanized rather than impeded a remarkable coalition and collaboration among some ninety countries.

In sum, critics of U.S. foreign policy typically use the unilateral label to discredit policies they disagree with, rather than arguing frontally against them. In fact, U.S. policies have more often been multilateral than unilateral in their formulation, although sometimes implementation has involved fewer multilateral contributions than might have been hoped. Finally, and perhaps counterintuitively, unilateral initiatives may sometimes provide an effective stimulus to promote rather than retard multilateral collaboration.

POSTAUDIT

The argument in this essay and its companion in the following chapters—that much of the inflated rhetoric about U.S. unilateralism is just that, namely inflated rhetoric—is as valid now as when this was written in 2002, although never previously published.

18. Whether Multilateralism Is Better or Worse than Unilateralism Is, Well, Situation-Dependent

IN FOREIGN POLICY PARLANCE, the media and the punditry typically view multilateralism as laudable and unilateralism—meaning a putative "go-it-alone" policy of the United States—as culpable. For example, during calendar year 2002, the *Washington Post* and the *New York Times* published 492 and 476 articles, respectively, carrying these terms and their corresponding spins.

This standard treatment is simplistic and misleading. Whether unilateralism or multilateralism is good or bad, appropriate or inappropriate, depends on the circumstances.

In some situations, unilateralism may be better because it provides a timely initiative that multilateralism would delay or preclude. The unilateral U.S. announcement in 2001 of its intention to withdraw from the Antiballistic Missile (ABM) Treaty in order to pursue missile defense more effectively is one example.

In other situations, multilateralism can be ill-advised because of its propensity to reflect lowest-common denominator temporizing. The Kyoto Treaty on global warming and emission controls is an illustration.

In still other situations, a policy that is unilateral at its inception may become multilateral and then still later revert toward unilateralism. The still-evolving policy toward disarming Iraq and removing Saddam Hussein's regime is a case in point.

In still other circumstances, bilateralism, or a series of bilateralisms—the so-called hub-and-spokes model—may be preferable for both the hub and the spokes. U.S. bilateral understandings with several European as well as Middle Eastern countries concerning the possible use of force in Iraq as well as its subsequent reconstruction are an example.

Consider these situations in more detail:

When Unilateralism Works:
U.S. Withdrawal from the 1972 ABM Treaty

After the Bush administration took office in January 2001, it announced its unilateral intention to proceed aggressively with a thin missile defense and to withdraw from the ABM Treaty, thereby avoiding the constraints in that treaty on the development of ABM technology. The decision, vehemently decried by our European allies, subsequently led to the Treaty of Moscow, signed by Presidents Bush and Putin in May 2002, calling for reductions in nuclear warheads by two-thirds on both sides by 2012, as well as possible collaboration between the signatories to accelerate development, testing, and deployment of thin national missile defense systems. This outcome was widely applauded by many of those who had sharply criticized the initial unilateral U.S. decision.

Where, as in this instance, success emerges from unilateralism, the conventionally negative connotations of unilateralism can be maintained by a convenient semantic adjustment: *unilateralism* is relabeled as *leadership*!

When Multilateralism Doesn't Work: The Kyoto Treaty

What was and remains a symbol of global multilateralism—the Kyoto Protocol Treaty on global warming—actually discredits that process or its outcome.

U.S. disavowal in 2001 of the Kyoto Protocol, which the Clinton administration had previously endorsed, is usually treated as a conspicuous and malign example of unilateralism. In fact, the episode exemplifies the sometimes-wayward consequences of multilateralism that, in this instance, produced a deeply flawed treaty—leading to unilateral U.S. rejection of the Kyoto Treaty.

The first flaw was, of course, the deep uncertainties about the assumptions underlying the treaty's provisions: specifically, the extent to which global warming has actually occurred, how serious it is, its attribution to human rather than natural causes, and its costs and benefits—matters effectively exposed and debated by the Danish statistician Bjorn Lomborg in *The Skeptical Environmentalist* (Cambridge University Press, 2001).

The second flaw was the added cost burdens that compliance with the treaty would impose on the U.S. and global economies, then as now experiencing weak economic growth.

Still a third flaw was the treaty's misconceived focus on *gross* CO_2 emissions rather than *net* emissions, which would allow for absorption of CO_2 by forests and grasslands. Focusing on the proper net indicator would reduce emissions attributed to the United States to very low levels.

And a final flaw was the treaty's omission of China and India from emission ceilings. Although their current emissions are relatively low, their prospective emissions are likely to be substantial because of their relatively high expected rates of GDP growth in the coming decade.

When Unilateralism Merges with Multilateralism:
The Possible War against Iraq

The U.S. animus against Iraq is based on two principal concerns: first, the threat posed by Iraq's possession of weapons of mass destruction and the technology to produce them and, second, Iraq's current and potential support for international terrorism. Although there is substantial evidence underlying both of these concerns, the evidence that has been publicly available is insufficient to convince much of the international community.

Nevertheless, the Bush administration has managed to link its own unilateral convictions of the validity of these concerns with multilateral efforts to remove the threat posed by Iraq. Reflecting this strategy, both Houses of the U.S. Congress enacted, on October 10 and 11, 2002, by overwhelming majorities, "authorization for the use of U.S. military force against Iraq."

The unilateral U.S. measure decisively influenced and expedited the often-dilatory multilateral processes of the United Nations Security Council, resulting in the council's unanimous endorsement, on November 8, 2002, of a resolution establishing a new UN commission to monitor, verify, and inspect all areas of Iraq with a view to removing or destroying any weapons of mass destruction in Iraq's possession. If Iraq commits a "material breach" of its obligations under the resolution, the council will "convene immediately" to consider further actions.

Although the unilateral U.S. authorization to use force was crucial in enactment of the Security Council resolution, the content of the resolution differs from that of the congressional authorization in two fundamental ways: first, in describing Iraq's threat to international security, the congressional authorization cites both the threat posed by Iraq's weapons of mass destruction and its prior and continued support for al-Qaeda and international terrorism, whereas the Security Council resolution omits any reference to Iraq's support for terrorism; second, the Security Council resolution does not authorize the use of force, opting instead to "convene immediately" if anything less than full compliance is forthcoming from Iraq.

How this situation will play out is uncertain. There are several plausible scenarios in this evolving interaction between unilateralism and multilateralism, including (1) manifest noncompliance by Iraq that would trigger an immediate council resolution for collective military action to disarm Iraq; (2) a decision by the United States that, although the Security Council may be dilatory or reluctant to act, the evidence of "material breaches" is sufficient to precipitate unilateral U.S. military intervention; and (3) same as (2), except that, along with U.S. forces, several other coalition members, including the United Kingdom, Turkey, Qatar, Kuwait, Saudi Arabia, Oman, Bahrain, Romania, and probably others would provide supporting forces and facilities.

Among these possible scenarios, the first and second might be termed *pure multilateralism* and *pure unilateralism*, respectively, whereas the third would be a hybrid—partly unilateral, partly multilateral—a "coalitional" outcome.

When the Mix between Unilateralism and Multilateralism Takes the "Hub-and-Spokes" Form

More frequently than either pure multilateralism or pure unilateralism, U.S. foreign policies entail bilateral efforts with other countries. This "hub-and-spokes" model typically characterizes U.S. security arrangements and operations with Japan, Korea, and Israel, and, in the evolving Iraq situation, with Britain, Turkey, Qatar, Kuwait, Saudi Arabia, and Romania. Although the U.S. role as a hub is singular, these bilateral undertakings are certainly *not* unilateral.

What these illustrations demonstrate is that reality is more complex than is encompassed by designating multilateralism as good and unilateralism as bad; depending on the circumstances either may be preferable to the other. In this more complex reality, U.S. security policies typically are more differentiated and nuanced than is suggested by the usual normative distinction between the two.

POSTAUDIT

Written at the end of 2002, the suggestion that sometimes unilateralism may be preferable to multilateralism as well that, in other cases, the reverse may apply, and that in other situations hybrid forms may be more advantageous, still makes good sense five years later. The examples that are cited, however—particularly concerning Iraq—are less timely, therefore somewhat downgrading the value of the essay.

19. Traditional Allies Are Not Permanent Allies

MID-NINETEENTH-CENTURY BRITAIN, although not hegemonic, was "first among equals" in the global power balance. Its then foreign minister and future prime minister, Lord Palmerston, asserted a proposition about Britain's "interests" and allies that is remarkably relevant to the global position of the United States today.

Palmerston asserted that "we have no eternal allies and we have no perpetual enemies," but that Britain's "interests are eternal and perpetual."

To make Palmerston's proposition relevant to the U.S. position today requires a modest adjustment and some further elaboration. Changing circumstances can change national interests: for example, progress in weapons technology as well as in the techniques of terrorism have altered America's vital interests. In the twenty-first century these interests include, as they have not in the past, preventing proliferation of weapons of mass destruction to other nations and especially preventing acquisition of such

A slightly edited version was published in the *International Herald Tribune* on July 7, 2004, under the title "A Test to Determine Who's an Ally."

weapons by terrorists within or outside the jurisdictions of nation-states.

Furthermore, in the flux and diversity of today's world, Palmerston's dichotomy between allies and enemies is insufficient to describe the shifting stances that other countries adopt toward the United States and that the United States adopts in response. Frequent references by pundits, scholars, and policymakers to America's "traditional allies"—notably France and Germany—are hardly adequate or accurate in characterizing where, when, and why these and other countries ally with, or distance themselves from, the United States or actively oppose it on major security and foreign policy issues.

On some of these issues France and Germany align with the United States. Intervention in Afghanistan and combating international terrorism are examples. On other issues, these "traditional allies" directly and vociferously oppose policies proposed or adopted by the United States. Besides the well-publicized instances of their sharp opposition to U.S. policies relating to Iraq and North Korea, a less conspicuous but significant example is the embargo on sales to China of advanced conventional weapons (such as attack aircraft and medium-range missiles). Concern for a possible reprise of the 1996 crisis in the Taiwan Strait has led the United States to urge that this embargo—originally imposed jointly by the European Union and the United States after the Tiananmen massacre of 1989—should be maintained, notwithstanding the particularly close and cooperative relations that the United States currently has with China. Contrariwise, France has recently urged the EU to abandon the embargo.

A simple litmus test provides a good fix on which countries generally and predictably, if not "perpetually," align with the United States, which do not, and which fluctuate between one stance and the other. Underlying the test is the cardinal principle that defines an alliance: allies recognize and acknowledge that they share major common interests, whether or not these are incorporated in a formal document. These shared interests constitute so-called collective goods, whose importance to the allies warrant their commitment to share in the costs and other burdens of securing those goods. Precisely how alliance burdens will be shared is invariably and inevitably subject to negotiations rather than being integral to the alliance.

Consider the following seven current and major international security issues; U.S. interests, policies, and pronouncements on all of them are clear and unequivocal:

- Countering global terrorism

- Committing to security, reconstruction, and democratization in Iraq

- Committing to security, reconstruction, and democratization in Afghanistan

- Promoting a two-state "road map" solution to the Israel-Palestine conflict, while maintaining strong support for Israel

- Insisting on multilateral negotiations by the six powers (rather than unilateral negotiations by the United States) for the elimination of North Korea's nuclear programs and capabilities

- Endorsing a peaceful resolution to Taiwan's status through negotiations between the parties, while opposing provocative moves by Taiwan as well as the use of force by the mainland

- Demanding that Iran be inspected and monitored to assure that it forgoes nuclear weapons development

Now, consider which countries support or oppose these U.S. policies or, instead, adopt a stance of neutrality toward them. When this test is applied to the seven issues, it is perhaps not surprising to find that the policies and behaviors of Britain, Australia, Japan, and South Korea display a strong alignment with the United States on at least five of these issues. On two of the issues—Taiwan and Israel-Palestine—the four countries incline toward more neutral stances than that of the United States.

What is more surprising is that the policies and behaviors of China, India, Pakistan, and Russia are more closely aligned with U.S. policies and interests than are those of France and Germany! Of the seven issues in this simple test, China, India, Pakistan, and Russia support the U.S. stance to an equal or greater extent than do France and Germany and oppose no more of the U.S. positions nor incline toward neutrality with respect to more of them, than do our so-called traditional allies!

One prescient implication of Palmerston's original proposition is as relevant today as it was in Palmerston's time: it is important to update and reclassify countries as allies or adversaries or something in between because traditional alignments with or against the United States are neither perpetual nor eternal.

POSTAUDIT

In the years since this was written, it can be argued that South Korea and Russia have perhaps distanced themselves farther from the United States, while France and Germany have moved somewhat closer. Apart from this qualification, the basic position presented in the piece, as well as its conclusion, remains sound.

20. The Principal Global Imbalance Lies Elsewhere

NUMEROUS COMMENTATORS, including economists as well as pundits, both in the United States and abroad, vie with one another in proclaiming the unsustainability of the U.S. current account deficit—the excess of U.S. payments for imports of goods and services, over revenues from corresponding exports. They then often criticize America's unilateralism for ignoring this imbalance, combining the criticism with warnings that continued neglect may trigger a global depression if and when other countries choose to discontinue their willingness to accept dollar assets in compensation for the U.S. current account deficit. If, instead, the foreign holders of these dollar assets decide to liquidate some of them, then a drastic collapse in the dollar's value and a worldwide depression may ensue.

In fact such a dire result is unlikely; the analytic underpinnings of the argument are flawed. A modest rebalancing of the U.S. current account deficit poses a much less difficult challenge for the economy and society of the United States than for those of several other key players in the global economy.

The U.S. current account deficit in 2004 reached an all-time high in dollar terms (approximately $650 billion); as a share of

U.S. GDP the deficit of 5.5 percent is the highest share in the past decade. Since 1995 the current account deficit has risen gradually, from 1.5 percent in 1995 to the 2004 share of 5.5 percent. In only one year of the decade, between 2000 and 2001, did the current account deficit shrink as a share of GDP; the biggest jump in the deficit's share of GDP occurred not in 2004 but in the year 2000, when the deficit's share of GDP rose by a full percentage point. This was a year when the GDP growth rate in the American economy was just below 6 percent. As a general rule, as the U.S. economy grows more rapidly than most of its trading partners, so also does the U.S. current account deficit grow.

Not infrequently, commentators in both the United States and abroad often delight in characterizing these deficits as "profligate American spending" (in the words of British economist professor Robert Skidelsky). In fact, the way national accounts are estimated, the U.S. current account deficit is precisely equal to the excess of gross domestic investment in the U.S. over domestic savings; conversely, current account surpluses that are maintained by other key economies reflect a deficiency of domestic investment in these countries relative to their domestic savings. Thus, the U.S. deficit could be reduced either by raising domestic savings or by lowering investment or a combination of the two; conversely, the current account surpluses of other countries could be modulated by raising investment or/and lowering savings.

It's worth emphasizing that the generally buoyant level of investment in the United States, which underlies the current account deficit, is in part responsible for the strong performance of the American economy relative to all other major industrial economies. In particular, high U.S. investment has fed a sustained rise in U.S. labor productivity and therefore of rising wages over the past decade.

The U.S. current account deficit is mirrored by current account surpluses in other countries. Specifically, the multilateral current account surpluses of four other countries represent nearly 60 percent of the global U.S. current account deficit. These four other countries are Japan, with a current account surplus of nearly $170 billion in 2004; Germany, with a surplus of more than $100 billion; Russia, with more than $90 billion in surplus; and China, with $46 billion surplus. If the U.S. current account deficit were to shrink in the next few years, the indirect multilateral consequence would be that these countries will have to import more or export less and to invest more at home and/or save less than they currently do.

A modest rebalancing of the U.S. current account deficit would be more comfortable and is more likely than would be the implied adjustments in the four major current account surplus economies. Several prospective changes in the U.S. economy are likely to point in this direction. An uptick in U.S. household savings is likely to ensue from several recent macroeconomic trends: for example, the emergence of health savings accounts in the health-care sector; the possibility of personal savings accounts as add-ons to Social Security accounts; and, perhaps even more significant, the spreading belief among the younger cohorts of the U.S. labor force that Social Security benefits may be reduced in the future, thereby generating stronger incentives among younger workers to save more themselves outside the Social Security framework.

On the other hand, prospects for the adjustments in the economies of the four surplus countries that would facilitate the U.S. rebalancing are more dubious, and their corresponding macroeconomic policies to move in this direction are more nebulous. Whether and how Japan, with a recent lapse in its low GDP growth rate, Germany, with a near-stagnant economy and a 10.5 percent unemployment rate, and Russia, much of whose 6.7 percent impressive GDP growth rate has been due to its oil-dependent export surplus, can make the necessary adjustments in their respective economies is considerably more problematic than are the requisite adjustments in the American economy. Indeed, among the four principal surplus countries, China is probably best situated to lower its current account surpluses in the next few years.

Ironically, even modest rebalancing of the U.S. current account deficit is likely to impose less of a challenge to the American economy than to the economies of other countries that have excessively relied on current account surpluses to either avoid stagnation (Japan and Germany) or to generate high economic growth (Russia and China).

POSTAUDIT

I continue to believe that the American economy can more readily adjust to a reduction in its large current account deficits than the four surplus countries can adjust to reductions in their surpluses. None of the changes anticipated in this piece, however—for example, a rise in U.S. household savings, slower U.S. growth or, indeed, a diminution in the U.S. current account deficit—has yet occurred, so the grade for this piece should be lowered.

PART FIVE

The United States

21. Doomsday for the Doomsayers?

EXEMPLIFYING THE SOMETIMES APT description of economics as the "dismal science," several well-known practitioners have been busily purveying bleak assessments of the American economy's prospects. The doomsayers include two Nobel Prize–winning economists, two prolific columnists of the *New York Times*, one of Wall Street's top financial economists, and several alarmist writers of the London *Economist*.

Their pessimistic forecasts include a double-dip recession, economic "flat-lining," or a U.S. reprise of Japan's protracted twelve-year stagnation. The pessimists are reputable folk, and they occasionally mobilize evidence in support of their gloomy prognoses. But to accept these forecasts would be a big mistake. Benign scenarios for the American economy are more plausible. As another Nobelist pointed out several decades ago, economists "have correctly predicted nine of the last five recessions"!

The difference between the dismal and the benign forecasts is important. It is a difference between annual U.S. economic

A slightly edited version was published in the *Wall Street Journal* on December 2, 2002, under the title "Doom or Boom?"

growth rates of 1 percent or less and 3.0 percent or more—
amounting to more than $200 billion in the annual U.S. gross
domestic product and more than 0.5 percent in the U.S. unemployment rate. This difference would have major significance
both for the United States and the rest of the world.

Forecasting is inevitably a hazardous business—to paraphrase
Yogi Berra, "It's dangerous to make predictions, especially about
the future." Economic forecasts are also hazardous because of
something in the economic realm akin to the uncertainty that
Heisenberg discovered in the physical realm: economists' forecasts may affect what they purport to be forecasting.

The elements of a more benign, even optimistic, scenario for
the American economy are numerous and powerful. They have
been neglected by the media compared to the emphasis and attention accorded to the gloomier possibilities. The favorable and
neglected elements include the following:

- The cumulative positive effects on corporate and investor behavior of continued and perhaps accelerated implementation
  of reductions in marginal tax rates, abetted in the forthcoming 108th Congress by reduction if not elimination of the
  anomalous double taxation of dividends. The current practice—taxing net income of corporations and then also taxing
  dividends paid to shareholders—impairs the efficiency of capital markets by encouraging corporations to acquire debt
  (because their carrying charges are tax deductible) and dis-
  couraging equity financing.

- A moderate weakening of the dollar resulting from "natural"
  market forces, rather than from inappropriate and ineffectual
  government intervention. A mild weakening of perhaps 5–10
  percent in the foreign exchange value of the dollar may occur
  as a result of the continued large U.S. current account deficit
  (about 4 percent of U.S. GDP), along with some slackening

of autonomous capital inflows into the United States that have hitherto boosted the dollar's value. A decline of this magnitude in the dollar's value would have a doubly stimulative effect: encouraging U.S. exports and strengthening the ability of American producers to compete with imports in U.S. domestic markets.

- A further economic stimulus can be expected from the combined and cumulative effects of monetary and fiscal policy. The short-term Fed funds rate, at 1.25 percent, is already at its lowest level in forty-four years. Also, federal deficits, at a level of perhaps 2–3 percent of GDP principally due to increased outlays for defense and homeland security, are likely to have a mildly stimulative effect without entailing the consequential risk of inflation.

- Improvements in the efficiency and reliability of equity markets and the ensured gradual resumption of investor confidence should result from enhancement of "sell-side" regulation in wake of the Sarbanes-Oxley legislation; enforcement of higher standards of corporate governance by the SEC; imposition of appropriate penalties on the perpetrators of past corporate malfeasances; implementation of several "buy-side" improvements, including increased as well as quicker access to more reliable corporate information; enhanced investor sophistication; and, finally, a burgeoning of new investment in mutual funds because of their tax efficiency in offsetting prospective capital gains against capital losses incurred in the past two years.

These elements of a more benign, even buoyant, economic outlook are numerous and formidable. There are others, as well. One of these is the continuing and dramatic rise in nonfarm labor productivity (more than 4 percent for the year), enabling continued wage growth without inflation and potentially contributing to increased corporate profits and new business investment. Another is the pervasive resilience of the American economy, including the flexibility of its labor markets and the important, if ill-defined, "animal spirits" of American entrepreneurs.

To be sure, none of this assures that these positive elements will overwhelm such negative ones as the erosion of $6 trillion in household and institutional wealth as a result of the punctured asset bubble since 2001, the accumulation of large quantities of household and corporate debt in the United States, and the laggard performance of the EU and Japanese economies. Moreover, besides these familiar downside influences, other imponderables may have depressing effects, at least in the short term—for example, war against Iraq, further terrorist attacks against the United States, or a possible meltdown of the Japanese economy.

Nevertheless, a bottom-line assessment is that the ingredients of a benign trajectory for the American economy are numerous and strong and have been largely ignored or underweighted by the media relative to the hyping of the gloomier forecasts.

Although the "dismal scientists" have been given more prominence than they deserve, rebalancing this distortion doesn't thereby eliminate the grounds for their concern. The remaining uncertainty lies between those who believe the economic glass is half empty and those who believe it is three-quarters full!

POSTAUDIT

The bottom-line forecast described here—that the U.S. economy was (from the vantage point of 2002) more likely to grow at an annual rate of 3 percent or more, rather than the forecasts of 1 percent or less suggested by the gloomy punditry of the time—has been strongly validated in the intervening years.

22. The Mythology Surrounding Energy Security

LIKE *HARRY POTTER AND THE HALF-BLOOD PRINCE*, tales about energy security abound in mythology and fantasy. The difference is that, in the energy security fables, the myths are unrecognized.

Although the energy mythology has been circulating for decades, it has been revitalized in recent months by a series of disparate events, including inflated oil prices (although the $60 per barrel price in real terms is still below the oil price reached in 1973), China's and India's booming demand for oil in world markets making them the second- and fourth- largest importers, respectively (the United States is by far the largest importer, and Japan is the third largest), the offer by China's national offshore oil company CNOOC to buy UNOCAL for $2 billion more than the bid from Chevron, continued turmoil in the Middle East, and the disappointingly slow revival of Iraq's oil exports.

One abiding myth about energy is that, because the earth's oil reserves are presumably finite, these reserves will be exhausted at some point in the future. Moreover, by matching currently

A slightly edited version was published in the *International Economy* in fall 2005, under the title "Energy Fables."

rising rates of consumption—especially the accelerating rates of consumption in China and India—with current estimates of proven reserves, an approximate date can be estimated by which reserves will be exhausted. According to a former U.S. secretary of the energy department, this date will be sometime in the twenty-first century. This would be a compelling story if it were true, but in fact it is a canard. The reality is that, if and when the growth of oil consumption seriously depletes proven reserves, the cost of extracting the diminished reserves (whether extracting them from shale or tar sands, or through tertiary recovery from buried crude deposits) will have risen to such a high level that nonfossil energy sources—such as nuclear, geothermal, hydro, wind, and biomass—will be exploited in preference to oil and other fossil fuels remaining in the ground. Consequently the last few billion barrels of oil will remain unexploited in the ground because extracting them would cost more than they'd be worth.

A second fable in the energy mythology is that energy independence is both vital and attainable. The truth is that America's dependence on foreign sources of supply is ineluctable, a fact of life that can be mitigated, hedged, and cushioned in various ways but not avoided. Even if the United States were to secure all its energy sources from oil and natural gas within North America, including oil from Canada's huge supplies of oil-sand deposits, the United States would still be dependent on the market for imported oil. Because oil is a homogeneous, fungible commodity, the law of one price (allowing for the usual differences in transportation and insurance costs) must prevail. Were the United States to embark on a policy of eliminating or even reducing imports of oil in an elusive quest for independence, it would still be imposing an extra burden on the American economy, and the weight of this extra burden would depend fundamentally on the external market. Thus, if imported oil were available at a price below the domestic price as a result of pursuing factitious independence, the magnitude of the resulting economic burden would be equal to the difference between the higher domestic price and the lower international price multiplied by the volume of total U.S. oil consumption. Similarly, if the domestic oil price were below the world price, the American economy would be burdened by a similarly calculated opportunity cost of forgoing oil exports in a vain effort to avoid dependence on the world market. This does not deny that continued R&D on competitive, less-costly energy technologies and more efficient, non-gas-powered and competitively priced automotive vehicles can be valuable components of U.S. energy policy. But the notion of physical and formal energy independence is a myth. Dependence on the international oil market is a reality that is no more escapable than death or taxation.

A third fable in the energy mythology focuses on "players" in the global energy arena who allegedly seek to "lock up" energy supplies by a variety of stratagems—for example, property acquisitions, pipeline construction, long-term purchase contracts, and so on—that will protect them from future possible energy shocks. China is currently cast in this bête noire role. This fable focuses on a deus ex machina whose prominence in the international energy market looms as an ostensible and potential "threat" to America's energy security.

Until the early 1990s, China was actually a net exporter of oil. Since then its import demand has steadily and rapidly risen, propelled by two circumstances: first, China's extraordinarily high average rate of economic growth, around 9 percent annually, for the past twenty-five years; second, China's policymakers' failure to pass on the full costs of rising energy prices to both industrial and household consumers. The result is that China is, as noted earlier, the world's second largest importer of oil (at 5 million barrels a day), approximately half that of the United States, and displacing Japan, which is now the third-largest importer. To be sure, there is an element of reality to this perception of China as a threat in the world oil market. As a major and rising importer, China's growing demand for oil boosts international oil and gas prices. But most of the imputed "threat" that the myth assigns to China is ascribed to China's activism in bidding for and acquiring oil and gas properties in Central Asia and Latin America, investing in pipeline construction, and negotiating long-term purchase contracts at stipulated prices.

The irony of this part of the fable is that such activism would actually have the opposite effect from what is ascribed to it by easing rather than raising downstream oil and gas prices facing the United States in international markets. The reality is that, as a large and growing energy consumer, China's efforts and interests in increasing oil and gas supplies help rather than hinder America's energy security! What the myth portrays as a threat is in reality a contributor to America's energy security.

When the mythology is confronted by the realities, a few policy inferences can be drawn. For example, if tax incentives are offered to encourage exploration and development of potential fossil fuel supplies, whether these supplies are located within the United States or outside should be a distinctly secondary consideration compared to their net yield. U.S. energy security depends on the costs of energy supplies, not on their location. Higher-cost supplies available within U.S. geographic limits contribute less to U.S. energy security than lower-cost supplies generated outside U.S. geographic limits.

China's "lock-in" long-term contracts for delivery of oil at stipulated prices may or may not be soundly based (depending on the outlook for world market prices and on whether the lock-in contracts are hedged). On other nonenergy policy grounds, such efforts by China may be sharply at odds with the other security interests of the United States. Specifically, contracts that assure

Iran of extra earnings may register negatively with respect to their effects on nuclear proliferation.

POSTAUDIT

This essay's disparagement of much of the mythology surrounding energy security is as sound now as when the piece was written. Nevertheless, the standard fable—that "energy independence" can and should be sought, that the world will run out of fossil fuels in a calculable period, and so on— continue to dominate policy debate on the subject.

23. Efficient Equity Markets Require Smarter Investors

CONTRARY TO THE FAMILIAR ADAGE, every cloud does *not* have a silver lining, although some do. The clouds cast by the recent freshet of corporate fraud and other derelictions have a brighter side that will improve the efficiency of equity markets in the future.

Among the acknowledged sources of brightened prospects are the recently enacted Sarbanes-Oxley legislation requiring CEOs and CFOs to certify the accuracy and completeness of quarterly corporate accounts and invoking serious criminal penalties including jail time for violations; improvements that have been made in the SEC's capabilities for rigorous yet sensible regulatory scrutiny of public companies; and the wake-up shock administered to corporate officers and independent directors to take their fiduciary responsibilities more seriously in the future than they may have in the past.

These developments, although important, are confined to the selling side of the market. More important, as well as less recognized as a stimulus to more efficient equity markets, is the

A slightly edited version was published in the *Wall Street Journal* on September 27, 2002, under the title "The Buy-Side Revolution."

buying side: specifically, the now-heightened incentives for investors to become more informed and knowledgeable about what they are buying when they invest. Efficient markets require participants—buyers no less than sellers—to have equivalent access to information, as well as the capacity to use it. When informational access is asymmetric—for example, sellers have it, buyers do not—prices will be distorted and resource misallocation will be the result.

The theory of efficient markets is one of the fundamentals of modern economics: one Nobel Prize has resulted from it, and several others have drawn from it. By strengthening incentives for investors to become more informed and knowledgeable, recent corporate malfeasances, paradoxically, should promote more efficient equity markets, improved resource allocations, and a more productive economy.

A recent comment by AFL-CIO president John Sweeney—not always a fan of efficient markets—is a cogent reminder of the direction of needed change:

> The sad truth is that American consumers can shop with more assurance of quality and safety at their corner grocery store than American investors can shop for equities in our stock market.

To be sure, bets with a longer-term horizon are inherently more risky than ones with a shorter term. But the principal reason consumers can shop with more assurance in markets for groceries as well as for appliances, vehicles, housing, and other durable consumer goods is that consumers are more knowledgeable about these products than they are about the products offered in equity markets.

Financial professionals scoff at this line of argument, contending in rebuttal that investment products are too technical and arcane for individual investors to understand as well as they understand consumer products and services. This rebuttal has limited merit, as well as more than a limited dose of self-interest associated with it.

Individual investors don't have to become financial professionals any more than consumers of health care (a major consumer service) have to become physicians. But it is entirely possible for investors to become sufficiently knowledgeable about investment products to ask the right questions and demand the information necessary to make better decisions in accord with their own preferences and judgments. The result will be more efficient equity markets.

Health care is no less arcane than investment, yet modern medical practice has been increasingly evolving in a corresponding direction. Intelligent consumers of health care need to know and understand such matters as high-density and low-density lipoproteins, triglycerides, hypertension, resting-exercise-and-recovery heart rates, and so on, to make more informed decisions. And physicians are now trained to convey to consumers (i.e., patients) de-jargonized information about technical matters, to encourage patients to seek second and third opinions, and to have patients share actively in medical decisions. Individual and institutional investors should require their financial advisers to do no less.

In the wake of recent corporate defalcations, and in view of the long-standing and pervasive informational asymmetries between buyers and sellers in equity markets, investors now have stronger incentives to become more expert and more current about the following types of technical issues that will affect investor behavior and, in the process, contribute to more efficient equity markets:

- The governance practices of companies in which individuals and institutions invest, or in which investment is contemplated: for example, the credentials of nonaffiliated directors, whether they are genuinely independent and free of conflicts of interest in their relationships with top management, and whether independent directors have dominant and preferably exclusive membership on the key audit, compensation, nominating, and governance committees of the board.

- The conceptual as well as empirical differences among corporate income, earnings, revenues, and profits: precisely how earnings have been measured in the past, whether recent and current measurement of earnings (of key importance for calculating price/earnings ratios) has been changed from previous benchmarks, whether earnings have been inflated or deflated (for example, by capitalizing rather than expensing such transactions as software replacement and equipment maintenance, recording revenues in advance for goods and services provided, or underfunding or overfunding pension obligations).

- The number of stock options issued or replaced, to whom issued and in what magnitudes, whether or not options are or may in the future be expensed (there are plausible arguments on both sides). Of equal or greater significance than whether options are expensed is the particular valuation method used for establishing option values (there are several reasonable methods with different effects on corporate earnings).

The efficiency of equity markets can be enhanced not only by rigorous enforcement of prior as well as new regulatory legislation but by effective standards setting and oversight responsibility to be exercised by the Public Company Accounting Oversight Board created by the new legislation and by improved regulatory scrutiny by the Securities and Exchange Commission.

All of these can help, but in the final analysis more-efficient equity markets depend fundamentally on better-informed and more discerning individual and institutional investors. Although the sell side of the market needs to be monitored, the buy side requires serious upgrading as well.

POSTAUDIT

In retrospect, the article is perhaps too uncritical of some downside consequences of Sarbanes-Oxley for the sell-side of securities markets. The focus on buy-side enhancements for efficient functioning of these markets, however, rings true five years after this was written.

24. Public Diplomacy: How to Think about and Improve It

(*coauthored with Brian Rosen*)

Problem, Background, and Context

Foreign Perceptions and Domestic Consequences

America has an image problem. The problem is global—even the leaders of some traditional American allies have found it convenient and politically advantageous to disparage America. But the problem is especially acute in the Middle East and among predominantly Muslim populations.

Polls highlight the depth and breadth of the animus. In December 2001 and January 2002, Gallup conducted a poll of nearly ten thousand residents in nine Muslim countries.[1] By an average of more than 2 to 1, respondents reported an unfavorable view of the United States (see table 1).

The prevalence of an unfavorable view in Iran is unsurprising

A slightly edited version was published in *Policy Review* in October and November 2004, under the title "Public Diplomacy: Lessons from King and Mandela."

1. Andrea Stone, "Kuwaitis Share Distrust toward USA, Poll Indicates," *USA Today*, February 27, 2002, p. 7A. The Gallup poll has not been repeated since 2002.

Table 1. Gallup Poll of Foreign Publics' Opinion
of United States, 2002 (in percent)

Nation	Favorable	Unfavorable
Lebanon	41%	40%
Turkey	40	33
Kuwait	28	41
Indonesia	27	30
Jordan	22	62
Morocco	22	41
Saudi Arabia	16	64
Iran	14	63
Pakistan	9	68
Total	22%	53%

because that country has had an adversarial relation with the
United States for more than twenty years. More troubling are the
results from ostensible allies. Only 16 percent of respondents in
Saudi Arabia, supposedly one of America's long-standing allies in
the region, held a favorable view; 64 percent reported an unfavorable view. Results from Kuwait were even more disconcerting.
In a country that the United States waged war to liberate a decade
earlier, only slightly more than a quarter of those polled expressed a favorable view of the United States.

A Pew poll conducted in the summer of 2002, which was
repeated in some nations in May 2003 and March 2004, reported
similar results (see table 2).[2]

Moreover, according to the Pew polls, opinions of the United

2. "Pew Global Attitudes Project: Nine Nation Survey (2004). Final Topline," Pew Research Center for the People and the Press (Washington, D.C.),
2004, 24; "Pew Global Attitudes Project: Wave 2 Update Survey (2003),"
Pew Research Center for the People and the Press (Washington, D.C.), 2003,
T-132-133; "2002 Global Attitudes Survey, Final Topline," Pew Research Center
for the People and the Press (Washington, D.C.), 2002, T-45.

Table 2 Pew Poll of Foreign Publics' Opinion
of United States, 2002–2004 (in percent)

Nation	Very favor- able	Some- what favor- able	Some- what unfavor- able	Very unfavor- able	Total favor- able	Total unfavor- able
Egypt	3	3	10	59	6	69
Indonesia	5	56	27	9	61	36
May 2003	2	13	35	48	15	83
Jordan	6	19	18	57	25	75
May 2003	0	1	16	83	1	99
March 2004	2	3	26	67	5	93
Lebanon	8	27	21	38	35	59
May 2003	8	19	23	40	27	71
Morocco	*	*	*	*	*	*
May 2003	13	14	13	53	27	66
March 2004	8	19	23	48	27	71
Pakistan	2	8	11	58	10	69
May 2003	3	10	10	71	13	81
March 2004	4	17	11	50	21	61
Turkey	6	24	13	42	30	55
May 2003	2	13	15	68	15	83
March 2004	6	24	18	45	30	63
Uzbekistan	35	50	9	2	85	11

Note: Undated rows are for 2002.
*Morocco was the only nation that was not surveyed in 2002.

States appear to have worsened, although in some instances the March 2004 results reveal slight improvement from May 2003.

Without accepting the reliability of such polling evidence, it can be inferred that opinions of the United States held by most of those in Muslim and Middle Eastern nations remain distinctly unfavorable.

This displeasure cannot be easily dismissed as vague and loose views held by those in remote lands whose attitudes and behavior

are immaterial to the United States. It may not foreshadow ca-
lamitous outcomes for the United States, but it hardly provides
reassurance that such outcomes will not ensue. As one influential
member of Congress observed, "The perceptions of foreign publics have domestic consequences."[3] This is especially so when
those foreign publics and the behavior of the nations in which
they reside are having increasing effects on U.S. national security.

Charlotte Beers, the former undersecretary of state for public
diplomacy and public affairs, summarized the potential consequences of Middle Eastern antipathy toward America.

> We are talking about millions of ordinary people, a huge num-
> ber of whom have gravely distorted, but carefully cultivated
> images of us—images so negative, so weird, so hostile that I can
> assure you a young generation of terrorists is being created. The
> gap between who we are and how we wish to be seen, and how
> we are in fact seen, is frighteningly wide.[4]

That gap must close. President George W. Bush plainly stated
the task, "We have to do a better job of telling our story."[5] That
is the job of public diplomacy.

What Is Public Diplomacy?

The Department of State defines "public diplomacy" as "govern-
ment-sponsored programs intended to inform or influence public
opinion in other countries."[6]

The term was first used in 1965 by Edmund Gullion, a career

3. Dr. R. S. Zaharna, "American Public Diplomacy and the Islamic and
Arab World: A Communication Update & Assessment," Panel Two of a Hearing
of the Senate Foreign Relations Committee, February 27, 2003 (quoting Henry
Hyde).

4. Charlotte L. Beers, Hearing on American Public Diplomacy and Islam,
Committee on Foreign Relations, United States Senate, February 27, 2003.

5. Zaharna (quoting George W. Bush).

6. U.S. Department of State Dictionary of International Relations terms,
1987, p. 85.

foreign service diplomat and subsequently dean of the Fletcher School of Law and Diplomacy at Tufts University, in connection with the establishment at the Fletcher School of the Edward R. Murrow Center for Public Diplomacy. At that time the Murrow Center's institutional brochure stated that:

> public diplomacy . . . deals with the influence of public attitudes on the formation and execution of foreign policies. It encompasses dimensions of international relations beyond traditional diplomacy . . . [including] the cultivation by governments of public opinion in other countries; the interaction of private groups and interests in one country with those of another . . . [and] the transnational flow of information and ideas.[7]

Government efforts—sometimes though not always successful—to distinguish public diplomacy from propaganda contend that diplomacy always deals with "the known facts," whereas propaganda is typically based on some combination of falsehoods and untruths mixed in with facts.[8]

Other formulations frequently define public diplomacy by what it is *not*. For example, the planning group for integration of the U.S. Information Agency into the Department of State in 1997 distinguished "public diplomacy" from "public affairs" in the following terms:

> Public affairs is [*sic*] the provision of information to the public, press, and other institutions concerning the goals, policies and activities of the U.S. government. The thrust of public affairs is to inform the domestic audience . . . [whereas] public diplomacy seeks to promote the national interest of the United States through understanding, informing, and influencing foreign audiences.

---

7. "What Is Public Diplomacy?" See www.publicdiplomacy.org/1.htm.

8. See references to U.S. Information Agency, Edward Murrow testimony before congressional committees and other sources cited in ibid., www.publicdiplomacy.org/1.htm, 2002.

The semantic niceties of these multiple distinctions recall the hairsplitting of sixteenth-century theology. Indeed, the tasks of public diplomacy and of public affairs converge more than their definitions imply. The provision of information intended for domestic audiences is frequently received by foreign audiences as well; conversely, information intended for foreign audiences is also accessible to domestic ones.

Another formulation of public diplomacy in terms of what it is *not*—intended by this commentator to be critical if not dismissive—asserts that

> United States public diplomacy is neither public nor diplomatic. First, the government—not the broader American public—has been the main messenger to a world that is mightily suspicious of it. Further, the State Department, which oversees most efforts, seems to view public diplomacy not as a dialogue but as a one-sided exercise—America speaking at the world.[9]

Public diplomacy (PD) can perhaps be better defined by contrasting its principal characteristics with those of "official diplomacy" (OD). First, PD is *transparent* and widely disseminated, whereas OD is (apart from occasional leaks) *opaque* and its dissemination narrowly confined. Second, PD is transmitted by governments to wider or, in some cases selected "publics" (for example, those in the Middle East or in the Muslim world),[10] whereas OD is transmitted by governments to other governments. Third, the themes and issues with which OD is concerned relate to the behavior and policies of governments, whereas the themes and issues with which PD is concerned relate to the attitudes and behaviors of publics.

Of course, these publics may be influenced by explaining to

9. See Michael Holtzman, *New York Times*, October 4, 2003.
10. Whether this presumed governmental exclusivity in transmission should be altered is another question to be considered below.

them the sometimes misunderstood policies and behavior of the U.S. government. Additionally, to the extent that the behavior and policies of foreign governments are affected by the behavior and attitudes of its citizens, PD may affect governments by influencing their citizens.

In this essay we consider how to inform and persuade foreign publics that the ideals that Americans cherish—such as pluralism, freedom, and democracy—are fundamental human values that will resonate and should be pursued in their own countries. Associated with this consideration are two questions that are rarely addressed in most discussions of PD: (1) Should the U.S. government be the only, or even the main, transmitter of public diplomacy's content, rather than sharing this function with such other potential transmitters as nongovernmental (nonprofit) organizations and responsible business, labor, and academic entities? and (2) Should PD transmissions and transactions be viewed and conducted to encourage dialogue or "multilogue" (for example, through call-ins, debates, structured "cross fires"), rather than as a monologue through one-way transmission by the United States?

Purpose and Motivation: Private Goods and Public Goods

Four linked propositions—each of questionable validity—have, implicitly or explicitly, motivated the United States to energize and improve its "public diplomacy." Partly reflecting these propositions, Newton Minow has forcefully advocated the need for this improvement:[11]

1. The prevalence of anti-Americanism abroad—especially but not exclusively in the Middle East and among Muslims more generally—is partly due to the inability of "the United States government to get its message of freedom and democracy out

11. See his eloquent "Whisper of America" lecture, Loyola University Chicago, March 19–20, 2002.

to the one billion Muslims in the world . . . [and] to explain itself to the world."[12]

2. Lack of success in conveying the U.S. message has ensued despite the fact that "our film, television, and computer software industries dominate these markets worldwide."

3. A potential remedy for the failure of our public diplomacy may be found in the "American marketing talent [for] . . . successfully selling Madonna's music, Pepsi-Cola and Coca-Cola, Michael Jordan's shoes and McDonald's hamburgers around the world."[13]

4. Linking these propositions, it might be inferred that America's "marketing talent" should enable our "public diplomacy—the process of explaining and advocating American values to the world"[14]—to be more effective in combating anti-Americanism and promoting more positive views of the United States.

The foregoing argument is deeply flawed. It is fanciful to believe that redeploying American "marketing talent" would enable the $62 million appropriated to launch a new Middle East television network[15] to significantly diminish the prevalence of anti-Americanism.

The preceding argument suffers from three fundamental flaws. The first arises from the conflation of *private goods* and *public (or collective) goods*, and the inference that what works in marketing private goods will be effective in marketing public goods. In fact, marketing efforts and marketing skills attuned to and grandly

12. Ibid. pp. 12–13.
13. Ibid. p. 13.
14. The quotation is from *RAND Items*, August 22, 2002.
15. David Shelby, "Satellite Station Scheduled to Be Launched in Late December," *Federal Information and News Dispatch*, September 25, 2003.

successful in promoting the former may be ill-adapted to promote the latter.

Madonna's music and McDonald's hamburgers are private goods whose marketing can describe and evoke a personal experience. Individual consumers can readily connect with these products by seeing, listening, feeling, tasting, and smelling to test whether his or her reactions are positive or negative. Where private goods are under scrutiny, each consumer can decide for herself apart from what others decide or prefer. Empirical validation is accessible at low cost.

But these attributes of private goods sharply differentiate them from such public goods as democracy, tolerance, the rule of law, and, more generally, American values and the "American story." Instead, the meaning, quality, and benefits associated with these public goods largely depend on a high degree of understanding, acceptance, adoption, and practice by *others*, rather than by individuals acting alone. For example, one person's valuation of tolerance depends to a considerable extent on its reciprocal acceptance, valuation, and practice by others. Not only are these public goods "nonrivalrous"[16], but realization of *individual* benefits from them depends on their *collective* adoption (consumption) by all, or at least by the larger group of which the individual is a part. And the benefits of these collective goods, once the goods are provided, are accessible to others without imposing any additional costs on them. Beneficiaries of private goods pay incrementally for the benefits they receive. Beneficiaries of public goods do not.

Acceptance and support (including funding) for private goods depends on purchases of discrete amounts of these goods by individual consumers at market-based prices. Acceptance and sup-

---

16. Rivalry in consumption means that consumption of a private good by one consumer subtracts from consumption of that same good by another.

Table 3 Comparing Private Goods and Public Goods

	Private Goods (e.g., Madonna's music, McDonald's hamburgers)	*Public Goods* (e.g., U.S. values, interests, the American "story")
Conditions of Supply (Production)	Many competing suppliers	Single or few producers (principally government, sometimes also NGOs or others via outsourcing)
Conditions of Demand	Consumption of separate units by individual consumers	Collective consumption by members of constituency group
Support and Financing	Market-based prices charged to consumers' individual purchases	Collectively based and accepted by constituency, or by sponsoring group (e.g., U.S. taxpayers)

port for public goods depend on other means, namely, on endorsement by a *constituent group* (hereafter referred to as the "constituency") whose members collectively share in the benefits of the collective goods and (directly or indirectly and sooner or later) can accept the burden and responsibility of their attendant costs. For a summary of the key differences between public and private goods, see table 3. Later we suggest the implication of these differences for the conduct of U.S. public diplomacy abroad.

Another key difference between public goods and private

goods is relevant and important for the conduct of public diplomacy. Because private goods are discrete and separable ("rivalrous"), one person's taste for and consumption of a private good does not require another to consume the same good. The situation is different for public goods, which must be collectively consumed (hence, nonrivalrous), or at least collectively purchased. Similarly, those who dislike a private good may largely insulate themselves from its distastefulness simply by refusing to consume it. Because public goods are collectively consumed, no one is shielded or insulated from them. Their availability to one beneficiary entails their imposition on all. An individual can consume a Madonna CD without anyone else doing so, but that same individual cannot "consume" democratic values unless democratic values have been collectively adopted and sustained.

This difference creates barriers for the potential consumers of public goods that the potential consumers of private goods do not face. A constituency group that regards voting rights, women's rights, civil liberties, and democratic values as collectively appealing public goods, may therefore face hostility from an implacable *adversary group* that regards this package as offensive public "bads."[17]

We discuss later certain Islamic groups that illustrate the respective designations of constituencies and adversaries.[18]

Such are the differences between public goods and private goods that methods and techniques for effectively marketing one cannot be presumed to be successful in marketing the other. Success in each of these arenas may depend on rules and strategies as different from one another as those that account for success in basketball differ from those accounting for success in football.

The second flaw is that among some groups, cultures, and

17. See below, pp. 133–135.
18. See below, pp. 142–144.

subcultures American values and institutions are already reasonably well understood yet intensely resisted and disliked. *Mis-
understanding American values* isn't the principal source of anti-
Americanism. The source lies in explicit rejection of some of the
salient characteristics of American values and institutions.
Women's rights, open and competitive markets, equal and secret
voting rights, let alone materialism and conspicuous display, are,
in some places and for some groups, resented, rejected, and bit-
terly opposed. When this hostility is mixed with envy, the combination can lead to violent resistance.

The third flaw is that some *U.S. policies* have been, are, and
will continue to be major sources of anti-Americanism in some
quarters. The most obvious and enduring policies that arouse
anti-Americanism are strong U.S. support for Israel. Much of the
Middle East views this stance as providing support for an already
strong, dominant, and overbearing military occupation, whereas
U.S. concern and support for the plight of the Palestinian victims
is viewed as halfhearted and grudging.[19] To explain, let alone
extenuate, U.S. support for Israel as actually a reflection of democratic values, tolerance, and the defense of freedom, rather than
a denial of these values to the Palestinians, may be an insuperable
task.

Nevertheless, public diplomacy may mitigate this source of
anti-Americanism. What we have in mind is not a concession to
the cliché about "one man's terrorist is another man's freedom
fighter." Instead, PD might emphasize the long history of U.S.
support for *Muslim* Bosnians, Kosovars, and Albanians in forcefully combating the brutal "ethnic cleansing" in the Balkans in
the 1990s. This support often placed the United States in strong

19. Consider the following characterization by Israel's own minister of justice
of Israel's home demolitions in the Gaza refugee camp: Israelis, he said, "look
like monsters in the eyes of the world," *Los Angeles Times*, May 30, 2003. Those
who support people viewed as monsters tend to be viewed negatively.

opposition to both Russia's backing of the Serbs against the Bosnian Muslims and to European reluctance to commit military forces in accord with Europe's verbal condemnation of ethnic cleansing.

Another part of the story that could be usefully conveyed to the Muslim constituency by U.S. public diplomacy is the perennial American support for Muslim Turkey's admission to the European Union, also perennially and vehemently opposed by the European Union, especially by Germany and France within the Union. Reiteration of U.S. support for an independent Palestinian state is a third theme that a suitable PD effort could appropriately emphasize.

As important as it is to communicate America's history of support and defense of Muslim populations, it is equally important to communicate the rationale motivating these policies. In these instances, U.S. policies reflected and furthered the values of democracy, tolerance, the rule of law, and pluralism. The overarching message PD should convey is that the United States tries, although it does not always succeed, to further these values regardless of the religion, ethnicity, or other characteristics of the individuals and groups involved. Highlighting the instances in which the United States has benefited Muslim populations by acting on these values may make this point more salient.

Convincing others that U.S. efforts to further these values are genuine, persistent, and enduring requires that those receiving the message believe that the values themselves are worthwhile, that they are "goods." Potential disposition toward U.S. policies can be divided into three discrete groups: those who accept that the values America seeks are goods; those who may believe that the values America seeks are not goods but who nonetheless see them as a means to achieve other core goals (such as personal or family betterment, improvements in health, education, skills, and the assurance of personal dignity) that are associated with the preceding values; and those who believe that the goals America seeks, as well as the associated core goals, are bads and would therefore reject the entire package.

The first group is sometimes considered to be the least populous of the three, although one especially knowledgeable observer has recently suggested that the size and influence of this component of Islam may well be larger than has usually been assumed.[20]

Those in the first category will be most receptive to the contention that U.S. policies are beneficial. Because they already believe that the values the policies seek are "goods," they need only be convinced that the policies really do engender these values. Convincing those in the second category requires the antecedent step of convincing the members that the values themselves are associated with goals that are valued by those in this category (e.g., opportunities for personal or family betterment, improvements in health, education, etc.).

These two categories comprise what we have referred to as PD's "constituency." Those in the third category are presumed to be beyond persuasion; they comprise PD's "adversary."

Thus, two tasks emerge. One is to convey and persuade that U.S. policies are pursued because they seek to further values that are already accepted by the audience, including Muslims in the Middle East and elsewhere. The second is to persuade that the values themselves have other derivative effects that are accepted as goods.

Hypothesis: Constituencies and Adversaries

Reflecting on the earlier discussion of the differences between marketing public goods and private goods, and relating that dis-

<hr>

20. See Bernard Lewis, "Democracy and the Enemies of Freedom," *Wall Street Journal*, December 22, 2003.

cussion to the previously cited examples of potentially promising public diplomacy themes, we propose the following "constituency/adversary" hypothesis to guide thinking and debate about PD, and the formulation and implementation of more effective PD efforts by the United States:

> Effective marketing of the public goods represented by the values and ideals America cherishes requires two ingredients: (1) an existing or identifiable *constituency* expected to be relatively receptive and more or less congenial to the content of the message to be conveyed by PD; and (2) an existing or identifiable *adversary* whose actual or expected opposition to the public diplomacy message can be directly or indirectly invoked as a challenge and stimulus to mobilize and activate the constituency.

The effectiveness of PD efforts and messages, and more generally effective marketing of public goods, depends on (1) appealing to the identified *constituency* by focusing on the goods and goals to be achieved; (2) explicitly or implicitly recognizing the *adversary* or adversaries standing in the way of the constituency's interests in the delivery of those goods; and (3) capitalizing on the tension between PD's appeal to the constituency and the adversary's resistance to it.

In some cases and situations, effectiveness may be maximized by focusing the PD effort on the constituency and ignoring actual or potential opposition by the adversary. Constructing or reconstructing hospitals, clinics, and schools in Iraq is a case in point; the appeal does not need to be highlighted by acknowledging the expected opposition of the adversarial group. Instead, PD can be advanced by ignoring the potential adversary or relegating it to only limited recognition.

In other cases, PD's effectiveness may be maximized by acknowledging—perhaps even anticipating—inhibitory and perhaps violent oppositional efforts to be expected from the adversary. In advance of, or in response to those efforts, the constitu-

ency can be mobilized to stand up for the public goods in
question. Training and equipping indigenous Iraqi police and
self-defense forces are examples: opposed by adversary groups
and sought and welcomed by the constituency.

We apply and elaborate the constituency/adversary hypothesis in the section below dealing with the case studies of Martin
Luther King and Nelson Mandela.

Learning from Past Successes

To test the constituency/adversary hypothesis, this report applies
it to past successes in two different contexts of marketing public
goods that are, or are close cognates of, core American values,
and doing so in adverse and at times hostile environments. Specifically, we examine the speeches and public writings of Martin
Luther King Jr. in his attempt to achieve basic civil rights for
people irrespective of color, and of Nelson Mandela in his attempt to end apartheid in South Africa.

To be sure, there are manifest differences between the
circumstances in which King and Mandela operated, and the conduct of PD by the United States. King and Mandela were individual charismatic figures whose public causes and public messages were intimately connected with their personal styles and
characters. By contrast, PD is conducted by, or at the instigation
of, a government or a governmental institution, although it may
be important and useful to devolve some of this responsibility to
nongovernmental entities.[21]

Despite the differences, the efforts of King/Mandela and of
PD share a linkage that may make the experience of the former
instructive for conduct of the latter. In both instances, the central
concern is effective marketing of public goods: civil rights, racial
equality, and the end of apartheid in the King/Mandela context;

21. See pp. 145–147 ff.

democratic values, open societies, and competitive markets in the PD context. In both instances the messages articulated by these highly effective protagonists relate directly and forcefully to the marketing of public goods sufficiently congruent with those encompassed in public diplomacy that inferences derived from the former may be useful in improving the latter.

The following sample of significant, high-profile public writings and speeches was assembled.

Martin Luther King

1. Address to First Montgomery Improvement Association (MIA) Mass Meeting, at Holt Street Baptist Church, December 5, 1955.

2. The Birth of a New Nation, April 7, 1957.

3. Give Us the Ballot, May 17, 1957.

4. Letter from Birmingham Jail, April 16, 1963.

5. I Have a Dream, August 28, 1963.

6. Address Delivered in Acceptance of Nobel Peace Prize, December 10, 1964.

7. Beyond Vietnam, April 4, 1967.

8. Where Do We Go From Here, August 16, 1967.

Nelson Mandela

1. No Easy Walk to Freedom, September 21, 1953.

2. Our Struggle Needs Many Tactics, February 1, 1958.

3. General Strike: Statement by Nelson Mandela on Behalf of the National Action Council Following the Stay-At-Home in May 1961, June 1, 1961.

4. Black Man in a White Court: First Court Statement, October 1, 1962.

5. Address to Rally in Cape Town on his Release from Prison, February 11, 1990.

6. Address to Rally in Soweto, February 13, 1990.

7. Address to the Swedish Parliament, March 13, 1990.

8. Statement to the President and Members of the French National Assembly, June 7, 1990.

9. Address to the Joint Session of the Houses of Congress of the USA, June 26, 1990.

10. Works from before and after his lengthy incarceration were selected.

For each work, data were collected on King and Mandela's explicit references to the following: the good (G) or value to be attained; the constituency (C) addressed; peaceful activities the constituency conducted or was urged to pursue (ACP); activities the constituency conducted or was urged to pursue that may or may not be peaceful (ACA); violent activities the constituency conducted or was urged to pursue (ACV); the adversary (A); activities of the adversary (AA); and negative remarks about competing leaders (CL). In addition, we summed and characterized as positive references to the good or value to be obtained, the constituency, and peaceful activities the constituency conducted or was urged to pursue $\Sigma(G, C, ACP)$. We have also summed and characterized as negative references to violent activities conducted by the constituency or encouraged for it to pursue, identification of the adversary, activities of the adversary, and negative references about or activities relating to competing leaders $\Sigma(ACV, A, AA, CL)$.

Summary statistics were generated for King and Mandela. Through the course of this study, a marked contrast was noted between Mandela's rhetoric before and after imprisonment. To better display this difference, Mandela's summary statistics were reported as totals and were bifurcated between those before and after imprisonment (see table 4).

First, a caveat. Special caution should always be exercised in drawing conclusions from a small convenience sample. Moreover, a simple tabulation of numbers of references, as in table 4, lacks any indication of emphasis or intensity that might be conveyed by the context.

Still, some results reveal stark differences between the approaches of King and Mandela. In every speech or writing, King made substantially more positive than negative references. In contrast, before Mandela was in prison, his negative references always equaled or exceeded the positive ones. After imprisonment, his speeches were markedly different. In each of them, positive references substantially exceeded negative ones.

Turning to the individual categories, the data suggest that King consistently and frequently referred to the good to be achieved as his main focus. In six of the eight works cited in the sample, the good to be achieved was referred to more than any other single reference category. With few exceptions, King gave little attention to the adversary, averaging only one adversary reference per speech, or to the adversary's activities. This contrasts markedly with Mandela, who, before prison, made an average of three or four references in each speech to the identified adversaries and their activities. After his release from prison, however, Mandela's emphasis was sharply reversed; his attention focused instead on positive references and on the constituency, rarely making negative references or even mentioning the adversary.

In addition to these general points, a closer look at the individual works suggests lessons that may be applicable to public diplomacy more broadly and to the constituency/adversary hypothesis in particular.

Table 4 References in Collected Works of Martin Luther King and Nelson Mandela

Work	Date	Words	Good	Constitu-ency	Peaceful	Nonpeace-ful	Violent	Adversary	Activities	Competing Leaders	Pos	Neg
King												
1	12/1959	1585	3	0	1	0	0	1	1	0	4	2
2	4/1961	7027	2	0	1	0	0	1	0	0	3	1
3	5/1961	2537	3	4	8	0	0	1	2	0	15	3
4	4/1967	6863	1	3	4	0	0	3	3	1	8	7
5	8/1967	1574	4	1	1	0	0	1	1	0	6	2
6	12/1968	1125	3	2	1	0	0	0	1	0	6	1
7	4/1971	6738	3	1	1	0	0	0	0	0	5	0
8	8/1971	7627	4	2	2	0	0	2	0	0	8	2
Subtotals												
Mean		4385	2.88	1.63	2.38	0.00	0.00	1.13	1.00	0.13	6.88	2.25
Standard Deviation		2902	0.99	1.41	2.50	0.00	0.00	0.99	1.07	0.35	3.72	2.12
Mandela												
Before prison												
9	9/1957	4534	0	4	2	1	0	4	6	0	6	10
10	2/1962	2005	1	1	2	0	0	3	1	0	4	4
11	6/1965	5582	2	3	4	0	0	2	6	4	9	12
12	10/1966	3199	2	0	0	1	0	2	1	0	2	3

After prison

13	2/1994	1607	2	2	0	1	1	0	0	0	4	1
14	2/1994	1996	1	4	3	0	1	0	0	0	8	1
15	3/1994	1158	1	2	1	0	0	0	0	0	4	0
16	6/1994	1847	3	2	1	0	0	0	2	0	6	2
17	6/1994	2667	3	1	1	0	0	1	1	0	5	2
Subtotals												
Before prison												
Mean		3830	1.25	2.00	2.00	0.50	0.00	2.75	3.50	1.00	5.25	7.25
Standard Deviation		1559	0.96	1.83	1.63	0.58	0.00	0.96	2.89	2.00	2.99	4.43
After prison												
Mean		1855	2.00	2.20	1.20	0.20	0.40	0.20	0.60	0.00	5.40	1.20
Standard Deviation		554	1.00	1.10	1.10	0.45	0.55	0.45	0.89	0.00	1.67	0.84
Overall												
Mean		2733	1.67	2.11	1.56	0.33	0.22	1.33	1.89	0.44	5.33	3.89
Standard Deviation		1466	1.00	1.36	1.33	0.50	0.44	1.50	2.42	1.33	2.18	4.23

Note: The numbers indicate the number of references—that is, explicit referrals to the subject of each column heading.

Implications and Concluding Observations

The preceding question highlights a dilemma facing U.S. public diplomacy in general and especially in the Middle East.

On the one hand, there is a risk that a new, perhaps more sensitive and tactful public diplomacy effort may be too passive and ineffectual because its strategy is to appeal to an overly broad constituency (embracing all of the first two categories of people discussed in the section above) and therefore perhaps appearing bland and trite.[22]

On the other hand, there is a risk of appearing combative and arrogant if the adopted strategy seeks to mobilize the more receptive constituency(ies) by aggressively identifying and targeting specific adversaries within the Muslim community.[23]

Identifying real adversaries both within the Middle East,[24] as well as outside it,[25] may hedge against the first risk, but would increase exposure to the second.

Yet this dilemma is perhaps too sharply drawn. Mixed strategies may be feasible with different emphasis placed on avoiding one risk without unduly increasing the other. Moreover, the effective mix may prudently change or alternate over time, as did Mandela's strategy and message before and following his imprisonment.

To translate and transfer to the Islamic Middle East the framework we have used in analyzing the King and Mandela experiences is feasible, although perhaps something of a stretch.

In both contexts the challenge that faced King and Mandela

22. This first risk might be called the "King risk."
23. The second risk might be called the "Mandela risk."
24. For example, the militant and autocratic Islamists. See Lewis, "Democracy and the Enemies of Freedom."
25. Such as some Europeans (especially the Germans and the French) who have adamantly and perennially opposed admission of Muslim Turkey to the European Union.

in the past and is now facing U.S. public diplomacy is how to formulate and transmit a compelling case espousing public goods: civil rights in the United States and South Africa in the King-Mandela contexts; open and free societies, tolerance, and human rights in the case of U.S. public diplomacy.

As in the United States and South African settings, Middle East ethnography and sociology are no less susceptible to distinctions among different groups of Muslims in terms of their acceptance or rejection of the public goods that the United States cherishes for itself and favors for others. For example, Cheryl Benard distinguishes among four ideological positions in the Muslim world.[26] Ranging across the right-to-left spectrum, they are

- *Fundamentalists,* who reject democratic values and Western culture, and endorse violence to resist these values;

- *Traditionalists,* who want a conservative society, and are suspicious of modernity, innovation, and change;

- *Modernists,* who want to reform Islam to bring it into line with the modern world;

- *Secularists,* who want Islam to accept a division between mosque and state.

Benard suggests that the primary constituency for a realistic PD should be the modernists. The secularists and traditionalists comprise in varying degrees intermediate and shifting groups[27] that, depending on the issue and circumstances, may join with the modernists. Fundamentalists can be consigned—more or less

26. This discussion is drawn from Cheryl Benard, *Civil Democratic Islam: Partners, Resources, and Strategies,* RAND, MR-1716, 2003; and Cheryl Benard, "Five Pillars of Democracy: How the West Can Promote an Islamic Reformation," *RAND Review* 28, no. 1 (spring 2004).

27. Ibid.

unalterably—to an adversarial role. Benard suggests they should be opposed "energetically." It can be inferred, moreover, that such energetic opposition can contribute to unifying and strengthening the modernist constituency.[28]

Other putative experts describe Islamic constituencies and adversaries in terms that are philosophically and theologically closely congruent with Benard's discussion, though their expositions tend to be vaguer and less programmatic than Benard's.[29]

As is always the case with discretely categorizing things that exist across a spectrum, it may be that the ideological spectrum cannot be so neatly cleaved into these four categories. There may be a significant overlap of traditionalists and modernists: people who are troubled by the problems in their societies due to a persistent rejection of modernity but who wish to retain traditional values. These skeptical modernists (or progressive traditionalists) may lean toward a desire to modernize Islam, if only partially or slowly, and nonetheless be suspicious of a fuller reformation. Depending on the tactics employed, if PD were to oppose fundamentalists too "energetically," the effect might be to repel traditionalists or skeptical modernists whose support may be valuable.

Here, the King and Mandela case studies illustrate potential effects of different tactics. The "Mandela risk" warns of stridently targeting fundamentalists in such a broad way that traditionalists and skeptical modernists also feel targeted and their support driven away. Following King's approach would counsel focusing not on the fundamentalists but on the goods the modernists and

28. Benard's program for "energetic" opposition to the fundamentalists includes the following: challenging and exposing the inaccuracies in their interpretations of Islam, exposing their linkage to illegal groups, demonstrating their inability to develop their countries and communities, exposing their corruption, hypocrisy, and immorality. See ibid.

29. See Jack Miles, "Religion and American Foreign Policy," *Survival* (Institute for Strategic Studies) spring 2004; and Paul Berman, *Terror and Liberalism* (New York: Norton, 2003).

maybe the progressive traditionalists seek. The "King risk," however, is that polarization may be instrumentally necessary and that failing to target the fundamentalists "energetically" may dissipate the sought-after galvanizing effect on the constituency.

However the risks faced by an overly aggressive or overly passive PD may be hedged, one general inference from the previous discussion should be repeated. It should not be assumed, as it sometimes has been, that the skills, techniques, and tactics that have been effective in marketing private goods will be applicable to and effective in promoting public goods.

That said, it is nonetheless important to recognize that concentrations of creative people and innovative ideas are not confined to the government agencies charged with responsibility for conducting PD. Marketing private goods is, as we've emphasized, very different from an effective and sustained effort to market public goods through PD. This proposition is quite different, however, from contending that government (i.e., the public sector) should be the only or even the principal locus of PD. Enlisting, as well as refocusing, the talents of the information-communication-publicist sectors and practitioners should be a priority concern for enhancing U.S. PD.

Nancy Snow makes the point forcefully:

> Public diplomacy cannot come primarily from the U.S. government because it is our President and our government officials whose images predominate in explaining U.S. public policy. Official spin has its place, but it is always under suspicion or parsed for clues and secret codes. The primary source for America's image campaign must be drawn from the American people.[30]

30. Nancy Snow, "How to Build An Effective U.S. Public Diplomacy: Ten Steps for Change," Address delivered to the World Affairs Council Palm Desert, California, December 14, 2003. In *Vital Speeches of the Day* 70, no. 12 (April 1, 2004): 369–374.

With these thoughts in mind, a few approaches—some new, some retreads—are worth consideration:

- The tasks of public diplomacy and the obstacles confronting them are so challenging that the enterprise should seek to enlist creative talent and solicit new ideas from the private sector, through *outsourcing of major elements* of the public diplomacy mission. Whether the motivational skills and communicative capabilities of a King or a Mandela can be replicated through this process is dubious. In any event, government should not be the exclusive instrument of public diplomacy. Responsible business, academic, research, and other nongovernmental organizations could be enlisted and motivated through a competitive bidding process. Outsourcing should be linked to a regular midcourse assessment, with rebidding of outsourced contracts informed by the assessment.

- It would be worthwhile to consider differing modes of communicating the "big ideas" of public diplomacy through debate and discussion rather than through the typical monologic conveyance of the message. Other modalities are worth attention, such as structured debates, call-ins by listeners, "conversation and controversy" programming, and live interaction among different elements of the audience, including members of both constituency and adversary groups.

- Current efforts to bring honest, unbiased information to people in the Middle East may provide platforms for implementing the foregoing ideas. Radio Sawa and Al Horra are publicly funded but independently operated endeavors of public diplomacy. They build off past successes of outsourcing public diplomacy through radio transmissions, but success in this medium may be applied to other media. Television is already under way through Al Horra but so too could be other media, through print and public speeches. Radio Sawa broadcasts popular music interspersed with news. An implicit assumption of its approach is that the listener will be more engaged by the music and news reporting than news reporting alone. This rationale is equally applicable to debates, call-in programs, and live interaction among different elements of the audience. Indeed, such approaches have the added benefit of using tools that directly reflect the goals public diplomacy seeks: open debate, free expression of competing and conflicting ideas, and participation by citizens with sharply different views. The conduct of public diplomacy can be enhanced by employing instruments that directly reflect the collective goods that it seeks. In this case, the medium can become the PD message.

Still, a reformed and enhanced PD should be accompanied by limited expectations about what it can realistically accomplish. U.S. policies—notably in the Israel-Palestine dispute as well as in Iraq—inevitably and inherently will arouse in the Middle East and Muslim worlds opposition and deafness to the PD message the United States wishes to transmit. Although these policies have their own rationales and logic, the reality is that they do and will limit what PD can or should be expected to accomplish. The antipathy for the United States that some U.S. policies arouse is yet another argument that supports outsourcing some aspects of PD. The message America is trying to sell about pluralism, freedom, and democracy need not be delivered by the U.S. government. The message itself may be popular among potential constituents who view the United States unfavorably, but if the government delivers the message, it may not get heard. Nevertheless, even if outsourcing proves effective, expectations should be limited. Although outsourcing may put some distance between a potentially favorable message (pluralism, freedom, and democracy) and an unfavorable messenger (the United States government), inevitably the two will be linked.

POSTAUDIT

Some of the key distinctions highlighted in this essay (for example, between marketing private consumer goods and "selling" the public goods represented by the American "story," between transmission by government and outsourcing its transmission by others) are no less important now than when this was written in 2004. Moreover, contrary to conventional wisdom about America's public image, in many of today's most crucial international relationships (for example, those between China and Japan, between India and Pakistan, between China and India, and between Israel and Palestine), the United States is regarded as a valued friend by the other parties who don't typically view each other in this light.

25. Liberals and Conservatives: Who's What and Where?

ONE OF THE FEW MATTERS on which Democrats and Republicans generally agree is the appropriateness of their respective designations as "liberal" and "conservative." Their affinity for these labels is ironic because the policy orientations associated with liberals and conservatives in American politics are the precise opposites of what the labels stand for in the rest of the world.

The contrast is sharpest in countries like China and Russia, which are in various stages of transitioning from what were highly centralized "planned" economies to market-driven ones. But the contrast persists in developed countries, such as those of Japan and Europe, as well.

In China most of the recent reform measures that abridge the central government's control of the economy are viewed in party circles, in the Central Party School, in the Chinese Academy of Social Sciences, and in the press as the result of "liberalization" policies, and their advocates are viewed as "liberals." These liberal measures include the rapid growth of the private sector, which

Published in the *Milken Institute Review* in first quarter 2007, with the title "Paradoxes."

currently accounts for more than 55 percent of China's GDP—a share that continues to increase because the private sector's growth is substantially more rapid than that of the state sector. China's liberalization is also reflected by wider opening of domestic markets through reduction of tariff and nontariff barriers, and by a growing if sometimes contested recognition of the crucial importance of private enterprise and by admission of private entrepreneurs to membership in China's Communist Party.

Another controversial issue dividing liberals and conservatives focuses on reform of China's health-care system. "Conservatives" urge that care formerly provided by and through state-owned enterprises should morph into a system largely dominated by government—essentially a single-payer health system. On the other hand, "liberals" express concern about the perverse incentives created by a single-payer system and argue instead for some type of cost-sharing and copayment by consumers in a restructured health system.

Vigorous opposition to these "liberal" measures has been expressed by staunch "conservatives" (sometimes called "leftists"), who instead favor reversal of these changes; for example, the "liberal" reformers are urged by the government press (the *People's Daily* in a recent editorial) to "stay the course and stiff-arm the leftists."

A persistent question in China's discussion of these matters is whether the top leadership of the Communist Party's standing committee genuinely supports these liberalizing policies or whether the policies result from forces—both internal and external—to which the leadership is reluctantly accommodating. When China's previous top leader, Jiang Zemin, articulated his "Three Represents" concept in 2001, which made capitalist entrepreneurs eligible for party membership, this "liberal" innovation was considered particularly surprising because it emanated from someone previously regarded as a stalwart party "conservative."

A favorite pastime of today's China watchers is conjecturing whether the current top leaders, Hu Jintao and Wen Jiabao, are genuinely supportive of liberalizing policies or are instead simply accepting some of them to diffuse pressure to accept more.

In Russia, also, vehement debates are under way between those who endorse the Putin government's expansion of government intervention in the economy—especially in oil and gas, telecommunications, and other key sectors—and those who vigorously, if vainly, oppose it. The government protagonists constitute the "conservative" side of this debate; its opponents are identified as "liberals." Among the vocal liberal opponents are several top officials from the Yeltsin regime, including former prime minister Yegor Gaidar and former minister of economic planning Evgeny Yasin, as well as a former top Putin economic adviser, Andrei Illarionov.

A central issue in the debate focuses on the economy's relatively high growth rate—its annual average since 2000 has been above 6 percent, three times that of the other G-8 countries. Russia's "liberals" argue that this is largely due to windfalls from Russian exports of oil and gas and the rapid escalation of their prices (according to recent RAND research, about 40 percent of Russia's growth is attributable to this source), rather than to sensible government policies. The liberals contend that growth would have been still higher if the interventionist, "conservative" Putin regime had opened Russia's domestic markets more fully to foreign as well as domestic competition and that the current double-digit inflation would have abated if some of the economy's sharply increased foreign exchange holdings (currently $250 billion) were used instead for imports of investment and consumption goods.

Stated simply, Russia's liberals want less government intervention and control; the Putin conservatives want more.

Although political labeling who and what is liberal and conservative is especially vigorous in "developing" countries such as China and Russia, it is no less manifest in developed, industrialized countries such as Japan and the European Union.

Consider Japan's recently enacted program of privatizing its postal savings and life insurance system (PSS). With assets of more than $3 trillion, PSS is the largest bank in the world. It is government-owned and has been government-favored and government-protected since its inception. Its privatization is the most dramatic reform undertaken by the Koizumi government, requiring a national election last year to overcome parliamentary opposition, including extensive opposition within Koizumi's own Liberal Democratic Party. Opponents of privatization were viewed and viewed themselves as "conservatives" and included much of Japan's large bureaucracy as well as large numbers of voters with long-standing attachments to and deposits in the postal system. Supporters of privatization were viewed and viewed themselves as "liberals" and included most of Japanese modern financial and business organizations.

According to a recent study by the Fraser Institute, to start a new business in Japan is twice as difficult—more time-consuming and more costly—as in the United States because of the plethora of licenses, clearances, and mandated waiting times required by government regulations. Those in Japan who deplore these obstacles are viewed as "liberals"; those who support them are "conservatives."

Similar alignments and corresponding labels pervade the economies and societies of the European Union. Of course, Europe has solid credentials for classical liberalism. Indeed, the intellectual roots of liberalism's emphasis on free markets, competition, free trade, and the benefits of entrepreneurship lie in the eighteenth- and nineteenth-century writings of Adam Smith, David Ricardo, and the Manchester School in Britain, and of Francois Quesnay and the Physiocrats in France. On the other hand, Europe has no less solid credentials for assigning dominant control to the state either directly through ownership of enterprise assets or indirectly as the principal regulator of privately owned or mixed public-private enterprise. Although the stature of Karl Marx and European socialism have been degraded by the sorry history of the Soviet Union, the welfare state remains a vital "leftist" antidote to classical liberalism in Europe.

One example of these historical cross-currents is the active resistance within the EU to terminating its common agricultural policy (CAP) of government subsidies to Europe's high-cost agricultural producers—a resistance that is likely to abort the Doha round of trade "liberalization." The "conservatives" who favor the CAP and other forms of protectionism appear to be stronger than the "liberals" who favor their removal.

The cost and delivery problems currently besetting Airbus and its preponderant owner, the European Aeronautic Defense and Space Company (EADS), provide another example of the conservative versus liberal stance in Europe that contrasts with U.S. practice. The dominant influence in EADS of shared majority ownership by the French and German governments accounts for such anomalous management practices as having two CEOs and two board chairmen (one each for France and Germany). These practices in turn are defended by "conservatives" such as France's president, Jacques Chirac, and its prime minister, Dominique de Villepin, and deplored by "liberal" business interests and media commentators.

Public policies frequently and perhaps inevitably involve a choice between relatively greater reliance on markets or on governments—each with its own putative strengths and limitations. In most of the world, those who favor reliance on markets are called "liberals," those who favor reliance on governments are "conservatives."

Reversal of these labels in the United States is a phenomenon whose roots lie in the intersection between the Great Depression in the 1930s and the huge expansion of government responsibilities initiated thereafter by President Franklin Delano Roosevelt and his administration's New Deal. In FDR's second inaugural address on January 20, 1937, he expressed his faith in "the innate capacity of government . . . to solve problems once considered unsolvable." The expansion of governmental responsibilities that followed in the immediate and later years encompassed full employment, Social Security, health care, education, market regulation, environmental protection, and national security. "Liberals" in the United States following the lead of FDR and the Democratic Party became identified as those who advocated this expansion. "Conservatives" sought or at least accepted the label of those professing opposition to it. That these labels are exactly reversed from the practice in the rest of the world is an anomaly, as well as perhaps another instance of America's supposed "exceptionalism"!

POSTAUDIT

Reversal of the usual "liberal-conservative" labels in the United States compared with the rest of the world is too deeply embedded in the rhetoric of American political debate to change. More careful and selective use of the terms, however, would help to cool and clarify a seemingly endless and often confusing and mis-characterized debate.

About the Author

Charles Wolf Jr. is a senior economic adviser and distinguished corporate chair in international economics at RAND, a professor of public policy in the Pardee RAND Graduate School, and is a senior research fellow at the Hoover Institution at Stanford University. He received his B.S. and Ph.D. degrees in economics from Harvard. From 1967 until June 1981, he was head of RAND's Economics Department, and thereafter was director of RAND research in international economics. He was the founding dean of the RAND Graduate School, and served in that capacity from 1970 to 1997.

Dr. Wolf is a director of Capital Income Builder Fund, Inc. and Capital World Growth and Income Fund, Inc. Dr. Wolf has served with the Department of State, and has taught at Cornell, the University of California at Berkeley, UCLA, and Nuffield College, Oxford. He is the author of more than 250 journal articles and the author or coauthor of two-dozen books including *Markets or Governments: Choosing Between Imperfect Alternatives* (1993), *The Economic Pivot in a Political Context* (1997), *Asian Economic Trends and Their Security Implications* (2000), *Straddling Economics and Politics: Cross-Cutting Issues in Asia, the United States, and the Global*

Economy (2002), *Fault Lines in China's Economic Terrain* (2003), and *North Korean Paradoxes: Circumstances, Costs, Consequences of Korean Unification* (2005), and *Russia's Economy: Signs of Progress and Retreat on the Transitional Road* (2006). He is a frequent contributor to *The Wall Street Journal, The Asian Wall Street Journal, The Wall Street Journal Europe, The New York Times,* and *The Los Angeles Times.*

Dr. Wolf's main research and policy interests are the international economy, international security, and the relations between them.

Index